BY CATHY O'NEIL

Doing Data Science (with Rachel Schutt)

On Being a Data Skeptic

Weapons of Math Destruction

The Shame Machine

THE SHAME MACHINE

THE
SHAME
MACHINE

Who Profits in the New Age of Humiliation

CATHY
O'NEIL

WITH STEPHEN BAKER

CROWN
NEW YORK

Copyright © 2022 by Cathy O'Neil

Published in the United States by Crown, an imprint of Random House,
a division of Penguin Random House LLC, New York.

CROWN and the Crown colophon are registered trademarks
of Penguin Random House LLC.

Library of Congress Cataloging-in-Publication Data
Names: O'Neil, Cathy, author.
Title: The shame machine / Cathy O'Neil.
Description: First edition. | New York: Crown, [2022] |
Includes bibliographical references and index.
Identifiers: LCCN 2021052960 (print) | LCCN 2021052961 (ebook) |
ISBN 9781984825452 (hardcover) | ISBN 9780593443385 |
ISBN 9781984825469 (ebook)
Subjects: LCSH: Shame—Social aspects—United States. | Blame—
Social aspects—United States. | Social problems—United States.
Classification: LCC BF575.S45 O54 2022 (print) | LCC BF575.S45 (ebook) |
DDC 152.4—dc23/eng/20211109
LC record available at https://lccn.loc.gov/2021052960
LC ebook record available at https://lccn.loc.gov/2021052961

Printed in the United States of America on acid-free paper

crownpublishing.com

1st Printing

First Edition

Design by Fritz Metsch

*This book is dedicated to
everyone trying to do better.*

CONTENTS

THE SHAME MACHINE

INTRODUCTION

—————

TELL FRIENDS THAT you're researching a book about shame, and you'll hear the saddest stories. This has been my life for the last few years. I've heard about every shade and flavor of it: zit shame, sex shame, math shame—dark memories dredged up from the high school locker room, humiliations at the hands of camp counselors, doctors, star quarterbacks. They flow together in my mind, into an enormous, communal underground pool of dread and pain, much of it brutal. It's hard to look at and even harder to make sense of.

But one evening, when the subject of shame came up, a friend of mine who's an art history professor offered something entirely new. "Have you heard of the Pueblo clown society?" she asked. I hadn't. And so she told me about a shaming ritual in the Pueblo nations in New Mexico and Arizona. In one case she described, clowns' bodies are painted with black and white stripes made from clay. Their hair, parted in the center, is bound in two bunches, which stand upright on each side of the head and are also encased in clay. The headpieces are trimmed with corn husks.

These rituals have many layers of meaning, she explained. They're tied to religion, and it's such a sensitive subject that participants are discouraged from discussing it with outsiders.

I followed up with Peter Whiteley. He's the curator of North American Ethnology at the American Museum of Natural History in New York, and much of his anthropological research has focused on the traditions of the Hopi. This tribe has lived in northeastern

Arizona for a millennium in fixed settlements, which is why the Spaniards, when they arrived in the sixteenth century, included the Hopi as one of the peoples they called Pueblo, the Spanish word for town.

The function of the shame clowns, Whiteley says, is to reinforce the norms and ethical standards of the community. In seasonal ceremonies, which extend over two days, the clowns dressed in clay-striped costumes perform in a plaza surrounded by community members. The premise is that they are children of the sun who come into the ceremony with no knowledge of society or human morality. In some of their early skits, they seem depraved, shattering the rules of decency and decorum. They eat filth from the ground, steal from one another, simulate sex. Since they don't know the rules, anything goes. But over the following day and a half, their understanding advances, and they seem to acquire the basics of ethical behavior. In short, they are taught to be more Hopi.

In the process, they teach people about what's acceptable, what isn't. "They are the great commentators of the world," says Whiteley. "They'll call out transgressive behavior." And for this they employ shame.

In one ceremony Whiteley recalls from the 1990s, the clowns acted like comical drunks, staggering and throwing bottles around as they ridiculed a bootlegger, a man known as Cricket, who was selling liquor within the community, which violated an established rule. The alcohol he supplied was a poison developed by outsiders, and it endangered the health of the tribe. The shaming Cricket received was intense, Whiteley says. "He must have had pretty thick skin." It sent a sharp message not only to him but to the entire group. Someone thinking about bootlegging would now think twice.

The clowns' shaming of community members doesn't end with the laughs and jibes. Later in the ceremony, both the clowns and their shamed targets can receive formal forgiveness. With that, the shamed return to the tribe in good standing—though always aware that the others will be keeping an eye on them.

A day or two of ridicule and then redemption. This was pretty tame stuff compared to the dark and painful stories I'd been hearing about. And next to my own lifelong battle with fat shame, it seemed like coaxing rather than bullying. The Hopi ceremony, as Whiteley described it, doesn't tell the transgressors that they're bad people, or losers, only that they need to make a course correction.

How the Pueblo clowns taunt their targets tells us something about the role of shame in society. It can be healthy, even kind (once you get past its sharp edges). To understand what's so healthy about it, let's take a look at an altogether different variety.

Ever heard of bingo wings? The term comes from Britain, where bingo is an after-dinner staple in retirement homes. When a woman wins, she'll shout BINGO! Raising her winning card high, she typically waves it eagerly—and this is where the scrutiny begins. Her movements draw attention to her arm, especially the upper part of it, where in many cases a jiggling pocket of loose fatty skin sways back and forth. That is a bingo wing in action. To the judgmental mind, it represents ugliness, which generates shame. It's also associated with another powerful source of shame, old age, and linked with women, who suffer far more body and age shame than men. Plenty of class shame also oozes to the surface. Rich people, after all, rarely play bingo, an activity popular with the middle and lower classes—folks so thrilled to win a prize that they wave their arms madly, exposing their bingo wings.

The cosmetic enhancement industries thrive on body shame. In their messaging, they make it all too clear that bingo wings, also known as "bat wings," are gross, something people should hide with long sleeves until they can excise them with surgery. This viewpoint, which feeds their business, is echoed throughout society, from morning TV shows and infomercials to grooming websites. It is so pervasive that many of us take it as gospel. "Unless you fly around at night catching insects," says *Blue Hare,* a lifestyle magazine for older women, "no one needs or wants bat wings. So what causes them and what can you do about them—realistically?" The answer is to eliminate these unsightly appendages. The cost for the surgery, known as an arm lift, or brachioplasty, averages about $5,000 per arm.

As I see it, the Hopi ceremony and bingo wings illustrate two contrasting faces of shame. The Hopi shame clowns send signals to members of their community, using gentle ribbing to enforce cultural norms. In the case of Cricket, the alleged bootlegger, they're saying, "Don't poison us. Stay true to the enduring values of our tribe."

The people they mock remain members of the community. The others know and care about them. They check on their progress and steer them away from their transgressions. Their shaming targets what people do, not who they are.

Shame is a policing tool, and it has been one since the first clans of humans roamed the savannas of Africa. According to evolutionary psychologists, shame—much like pain, its first cousin—shields us from harm. Pain protects our bodies, teaching us to watch out for fires and sharp blades, and to run away from angry hornets. Shame represents another dimension of pain. It is administered by a collective whose rules and taboos are etched into our psyches. Its goal is the survival not of the individual but of the society. In this sense, shame is borne of the conflict between an individual's desires and the expectations of the group.

Shame, by definition, is something we carry inside. It's a feeling, one derived from a norm, whether of body, health, habits, or morals. And when we sense that we're failing to meet these standards, or when classmates or colleagues or Super Bowl advertisements make these departures all too clear, shame washes over us. Sometimes it just feels bad. But the damage can run much deeper, hollowing out our sense of self, denying us our dignity as human beings, and filling us with feelings of worthlessness. Shame packs a vicious punch.

Stigma, another one of shame's close cousins, is a mark that we wear on the outside. It is a signal to the rest of society that this person misbehaves or is intrinsically abominable. Sometimes a stigma is carried as a physical indicator, like a dunce cap. Other times a single word will suffice, branding a person as an addict or a felon.

Shame and stigmas enforce taboos. And some of their work, from an evolutionary standpoint, makes sense. The shame of incest, for example, pushes humans to spread out and enrich the gene pool. In most societies, shame discourages antisocial behavior, such as hoarding food. Making sense of such signals is a survival skill. The shame denotes one's fragile place within the tribe or community. In a Darwinian sense, it issues a warning, which is received as a foreboding. This alert dates back to our early days, when the shamed could be shunned, or even killed. The dread of abandonment is so powerful that it can make us feel nauseous or suicidal.*

Drunk driving is a relative newcomer to the pantheon of shame. Even more recent is the shaming of those who ignore social distancing or cough into a crowd during a pandemic. We shame people who do not look out for the group. It is the fear of shame, in

---

*According to a useful definition, taken from Patricia A. DeYoung's book *Understanding and Treating Chronic Shame*, shame is "the experience of one's sense of self disintegrating in relation to a dysregulating other," where the dysregulating other is "a person who fails to provide the emotional connection, responsiveness, and understanding that another person needs in order to be well and whole." This definition makes it clear that shame happens, at least at first, within a relationship with others.

many minds, that leads people to value their membership in that group over their egos and desires. When it works, it discourages our species from following some of our worst instincts.

Many others have written about the psychology behind shame, the doubt and self-loathing, or the magical trick of removing shame from your deepest psyche (consider me a skeptic), but in this book, I focus on how shame is manufactured and mined. I analyze shame as a global force and show how it is wielded to harvest something of value from us, whether money, work, sex, votes, or even retweets. Giant sectors of the economy are organized and optimized to make us feel horrible.

The primary purpose of shame is to enforce conformity. This, I know, is a problematic word. It signals spinelessness, sheeplike behavior, the sacrifice of one's individuality for the collective. Worse, the conventions of the group we conform to can be flawed or unjust. In Nathaniel Hawthorne's *The Scarlet Letter*, Hester Prynne is forced to wear a scarlet *A* for adultery. This shame is her punishment, and a warning to other women to stay within society's strictures. Yet one of those norms allowed the male predators, in this case the minister, Arthur Dimmesdale, to retain their honor and standing.

It wasn't fair. Hawthorne's book makes this clear, leading readers to empathize with the disgraced woman and ultimately to admire her. In this way, the author prodded society to shift its norms—to redirect shame from the victims of abusive relationships to the perpetrators. His motive was not to push Hester Prynne to conform to the Puritanical standard, but instead to redraw shame's boundaries. These same dynamics drive social movements today, from #MeToo to Black Lives Matter. These shifting borders stoke heated conflicts in our society, because people whose behavior once seemed to conform—from ass-pinching CEOs to Daughters of the Confederacy—find themselves newly splattered with shame. This hurts. To protect themselves, people tend to take refuge with like-minded allies or to strike back.

In these cases, shame is ineffective, even counterproductive. Instead of enforcing shared norms, it casts people off. This occurs all too often. In its myriad forms, modern shame consistently flubs its unifying mission, succeeding only in delivering pain and driving us apart.

The shamescape is in constant flux but always brimming with opportunity. Whether the business model is to lead someone to buy a treadmill, get a nose job, click on an ad, pay for a useless degree, sign up for a high-priced diet, or vote for a certain presidential candidate, finding a person's source of shame is often step one. What does she hate about herself, and to what ends will she go to hate herself less? This is the central calculation of the shame industrial complex, which we'll tour in the first part of the book.

The key players within this punishing ecosystem run what I call shame machines. There are countless varieties of them, ranging from publicly traded companies to government bureaucracies. Individuals also play a role, whether through Twitter accounts or self-help infomercials. All of them dole out weaponized shame. Some are in it simply to make profits; others cow the downtrodden, denying them benefits or trundling them off to prison. The shame acts as a deterrent, a form of silencing control, a distraction and deflection from clear thinking. When successful, it leads its victims to resignation and surrender. In this way, they cycle through the ever-hungry machines in endless loops.

From addiction to poverty, a constant in these shame industries is the concept of choice. The guiding premise is that the victims screwed up: They could have chosen to be rich, shapely, smart, and successful, and they didn't. It's their fault and, yes, they should feel awful about it. But now they have the opportunity to right the wrong, to correct the problem and follow the prescribed route to redemption, which is almost always fruitless.

Over recent decades, powerful new shame machines have emerged. In the second section, "Networked Shame," we'll see how the digital giants enlist us to shame one another, whether for ugliness, bad taste, or any variety of political faux pas. The machine-learning algorithms of Facebook, Google, and others are continually optimizing to spur conflict among us. This drives traffic and advertising, creating fabulous profits. But the by-product of their industry, now the most valuable on earth, is a toxic flow of put-downs and ridicule. Their algorithms reward us, increasingly, for hating and demonizing one another, while also nourishing cancel culture. Our lives on these networks even disturb our mental processes, jangling our perception of facts.

It's a potent brew. But shame can be used in other ways too. Those who have experienced it personally understand its power and are perhaps in the best position to harness it for good. However, doing so usually involves an emotional journey, not unlike the passage through the stages of grief. The first stage is hurt. When shamed, whether for addiction, poverty, or illiteracy, people suffer and can feel worthless. And being denounced by millions on social media as a racist or a rapist can create cognitive dissonance, especially for people who consider themselves "good." A natural response is to cast about for a way to turn off the pain. This leads them to hide the shame, or pretend it's not there. Some even blame others, or seek out people nursing similar grievances. That second stage of shame, denial, leads to no end of hazards.

The third stage, which many of us never reach, is acceptance. This neutralizes the shame machine. A fat person (like me), after decades of misery, finally says, "Yeah, I'm fat. So what?" A gay person steps out of the closet. At this stage, the person sheds the shame, and the constricting web of lies, secrecy, and self-hatred that has sustained it, often for a lifetime. Such acceptance can bring great peace and an almost palpable sense of relief. (I should add that people can move backward on their pathway of shame. A single stinging comment can revive the raw hurt that shame victims were praying they'd left behind.)

Finally there's the fourth stage, transcendence. That's when people who have suffered shame, and then confronted it, shift the focus from self to community—and take action to dismantle the shame machine itself.

The journey of a man named David Clohessy illustrates these stages of shame. Clohessy's misery began in his childhood but didn't come to light until 1988. One evening that year the Missourian, then thirty-one years old, went to a Barbra Streisand movie with his fiancée. It was *Nuts,* in which Streisand plays a prostitute facing murder charges for killing one of her clients. During cross-examination, she reveals that her stepfather sexually molested her when she was a child.

The movie struck a painful chord. That night, while lying in bed, Clohessy experienced a flood of devastating flashbacks. A priest was grabbing him, overpowering him, climbing on top of him. For nearly twenty years he had buried these memories. Now they overwhelmed him.

During those decades, Clohessy was quietly and unwittingly inhabiting the stage of shame marked by denial. In his story, as he told it to *The New York Times,* we see the victim gaining voice and confidence, and increasingly calling the vast churning engine works of the Catholic Church's shame machine to account.

After the sleepless night in 1988 when the awful memories came back, Clohessy spent several months wallowing in hurt. How could he have suffered such abuse and done so little to resist it? What would people think?

Then, despite his agony, he progressed. The crucial step was when he acknowledged what had happened and concluded that he wasn't to blame. He had not made a bad or sinful choice. It was then that he confronted his alleged abuser, Rev. John Whiteley, an associate pastor in the farming community of Moberly, Missouri. In 1991, to the anguish of his churchgoing parents, Clohessy sued the diocese in Jefferson City. In his affidavit, he detailed his charges of abuse against the priest.

Many people, as we'll see, never get to the point where they confront their shame and stop blaming themselves. Clohessy was fortunate: After years of struggle and many hours of therapy, he gained his voice and his power. He was willing to share his story, because he reasoned that it might help save other children from abusive priests. He put shame behind him and became a leader in the movement. So in the early 2000s, when *Boston Globe* reporters launched their Pulitzer Prize–winning investigative series about abuse in the Catholic Church, Clohessy was a logical source.

In 2004, Clohessy joined the Survivors Network of those Abused by Priests (SNAP), the preeminent self-help group for victims of clergy molestation in the United States. He went on to become the national director of the organization.

Clohessy's path is the model for the final part of the book. For the first time since encountering the Pueblo shame clowns, we'll see how shifts in shame can create healthy opportunities. Sometimes gentle shaming can be useful in establishing new guidelines, like wearing masks or taking vaccines. In other cases, the victims of social or economic injustice can turn the tables on their persecutors and shame them for betraying their stated ideals. This can bring down abusive CEOs, lead to social change, and even overthrow regimes.

My goal in this book is to encourage this shift: We'll fare far better as a society, in terms of both happiness and justice, if we succeed in redirecting shame from its current victims, who are disproportionately poor and powerless, to people who are taking advantage of the rest of us and poisoning our lives and culture. By turning downward punches into upward ones, we protect the social good. That should be shame's eternal role, its raison d'être.

––––––––

You might be wondering at this point why I should be writing about shame. I'm a mathematician, not a psychologist or a meditation guru. My first book, *Weapons of Math Destruction*, was about the poisonous algorithms in commerce, banking, education, and policing that punish people, mostly the poor. I'd built many different types of algorithms, so I could see where the toxic ones clustered. I knew how to deconstruct and reconstruct them.

My expertise in shame is both more personal and more philosophical. Like just about everyone, I cultivated my knowledge of it from painful life experience. But only recently did I start to examine my life—replete with fears and self-indictments—as a function of shame. That led to a slew of questions. Who transmitted that shame? Who profited from it? I came to a deeper understanding of my decades-long journey after seeing it through the lens of shame.

For me, this picture came into focus a few years ago, when I was interviewing a schoolteacher. Despite earning sky-high reviews from parents, colleagues, and students, she had received a miserable score on a standardized evaluation. This was going to get her fired. Yet when she asked to see the formula by which she had been judged, she was told: It's math. You wouldn't understand it.

She was being math-shamed. It was a classic example of punching down. The powerful—in this case the school administration—bent her to its will by shaming her, first by trashing her work and then by telling her that she was too ignorant in math to understand it. As a lifelong math nerd, I was impervious to that genre of shaming. But I had been witnessing it for decades. I was able to examine it with a clear eye, because my own feelings weren't triggered by it. I could behold its power.

But in other areas, I was a victim. The outsider view of math shame contrasted all too neatly—sickeningly—with my fat shame. As I watched the teacher's math-shaming from the outside, I recognized my fat shame, the self-loathing that had followed me every step of my life, like a personalized thunderhead blocking the sun.

Looking through this lens, I considered the role of shame in human affairs—as a tool of repression, profit, and control. Then I started to see how an endless roster of shame purveyors delivered every shade and flavor of it, from the shame of addiction to the shame of ignorance, ugliness, and aging. I saw how they manufactured mountains of the stuff. What if everyone at the office was whispering that you smelled bad or had slept with the boss? What if everyone on the internet heard about it? Once shame was stirred, the shame merchants offered products or services—everything from bogus diplomas to online reputation cleansing—to alleviate its symptoms.

The research into this book led me to think about shame as an immense structural problem in our society. This pushed me to analyze it systemically. It enabled me not only to address the sources of my own shame but, more important, to delve into false assumptions I used to justify my own shaming actions. In the realm of shame, most of us are both victims and perpetrators. To avoid pain, or perhaps in response to pain, we habitually and automatically deflect it toward others. Both the diagnosis and the remedy, I found, are usually rooted in phony science, cognitive dissonance, and self-preserving flattery. In short, lots of unnecessary bullshit. We should wield this weapon more carefully.

My purpose in writing this book is to shine a light on both the shame we've been subjected to in life and the shame that we heap on others, often without meaning to or even noticing.

I want to be clear, however, that this is not merely a self-help book. The goal is much bigger and more collective: to encourage us, as individuals and communities, to dismantle the shame machines that have been having their way not only with our moods and psyches but also with our government and economy. This is especially important now, because these engines, more potent than ever, are poised to amplify their efforts exponentially.

The first step to battling them is to view our interactions with one another through the lens of shame. Once people identify the shame in their own lives, they can start to see how powerful companies and institutions are benefiting from it. And then it becomes possible, bit by bit, act by act, to turn the tables. Shame doesn't only afflict us, it turns out. It also gives us the power to fight back.

PART I

INDUSTRIAL SHAME

CHAPTER 1

TIPPING THE SCALES

was jubilant. On a gusty autumn day in Cambridge, Massachusetts, word arrived that I'd passed my "qual," or qualifying exam. This was a crucial step toward earning my mathematics PhD. With my doctorate halfway in the bag, I was primed to celebrate—by baking a batch of cookies. In the sunniest, most triumphant mood I went to the Get-N-Go, a bodega next door to my Somerville digs, for ingredients.

I knew the clerk there. He'd always been friendly. But when I placed the flour, sugar, and chocolate chips on the counter, he shook his head and said, "Why are you buying that? Don't you know you're fat?"

I felt as though he'd slapped me on my double chin. My heart raced; tears leapt to my eyes. I was speechless, but I knew what this was from experience, and from an early age: shame shock.

Much of the suffering from being fat occurs on a gentler and more subtle scale. It's the looks people give you in hallways and on airplanes, the waiter's uneasy pause before asking if you want to see the dessert menu. Those microdoses of shame keep low-level misery and self-hatred on a steady course. Shame shock, though, is an explosion. It often occurs when someone confronts you, head-on, about your deepest shame. When you're exposed.

At that moment in the bodega, all of the shame's poison coursed through my body, leaving me frozen, disoriented, in pain. In this state, I lost track of who I was. I felt worthless, a flop, unloved.

I gathered the ingredients and made my way out of the bodega without saying a word. Even as the initial shock wore off, I remained under its spell. During the aftershock, it felt as if I were sinking, and I desperately worked to right the ship—propping up my own self-worth. I was getting a PhD, I told myself. I had a boyfriend. I was kind to people.

Such counterarguments ping harmlessly against the edifice of shame and dissolve. Shame transcends mere logic and extends its roots into biology. It stirs up hormones, tightens the jaw, turns the stomach into knots, triggers pain receptors in the brain, and, all the while, pummels self-esteem into mush.

To a lot of readers, this may sound extreme. Many people never experience a powerful shame shock, or don't remember it too well. For quite a few, no doubt, the concept of shame might resuscitate awful memories from the past—middle school embarrassments, awkwardness in the mating game, a demotion at work. But this week, perhaps this year if they're lucky, shame may appear to hover safely at bay. Someone else's problem.

However, as we'll see in this book, shame is a quietly active force, even among people who cannot recall being recently shame-shocked and claim to feel fine about themselves. After all, shame—both in the giving and in the receiving—does most of its nasty work in the dark, often tiptoeing around the edges of the conscious mind. We tend to forget how bad it feels.

Still, whether it's a full-blown case of shock, as I experienced in the bodega, or deeply buried feelings of worthlessness and vulnerability, the crucial question becomes urgent: What did I do wrong? There seems to have been a choice, a fork in the road. Every healthy and self-respecting member of society followed the right route, and

I took the wrong one. Maybe I was weak, lazy, or stupid. Whatever the reason, I feel ashamed, because I screwed up.

The entire shamescape hinges on this idea of choice, which is usually false. Millions of us carry around the enduring pain of making the wrong choice again and again. We harbor an abiding fear that shame will explode, as it did on me in that Somerville corner store, and that we'll be unmasked as losers. And we hold out hope that by pursuing the *right choice*, we can free ourselves of shame.

My own story is a case study in how shame is born, how it's sustained, nurtured, and monetized. Fat shame conditioned my behavior, step-by-step, year by year. This is the journey that opened my eyes to the insidious dominance of shame in our lives.

It began forty years ago, when I was a pudgy girl living with her two overweight parents in a Boston suburb in the 1980s. Always big for my age, I was already the size of a grown woman by the time I reached fourth grade. At my Lexington public school, I was an outcast, the kid who got picked last for the team, who sat alone in the cafeteria. My size appeared to signal that I was a reject.

I suffered plenty of humiliations in gym class, but the most excruciating was the yearly weigh-in for the Presidential Physical Fitness Test. I remember standing in line in the gym for my turn to be weighed. As each child ahead of me stepped onto the scale, the nurse shouted out the result to the gym teacher, who wrote down the numbers on a pad. My classmates all seemed to weigh about seventy pounds. I was well aware that I weighed more than one hundred. As I stepped onto the scale, I bowed my head in shame—my face hot, my stomach in knots—bracing myself for the nurse to call out the embarrassing number. For days afterward, the other kids taunted me: "Do you really weigh that much? 105 pounds?"

Something had to be done. So at age eleven, I was ready and

willing when my parents told me I'd need to go on a diet. They sat me down and explained that calories were units of energy. If we could control them—making sure we ate less than our "maintenance amount"—we'd lose weight. Burn more calories than you consume, you drop pounds, my dad explained. Easy peasy.

The diet promised a pathway from shame. The implicit assumption was that from my earliest years I had screwed up by overeating. Given a choice, I had followed my appetite and selfishly opted for gluttony, one of the seven deadly sins. But I could return to the norm by shackling my hunger. All I had to do was follow the rules. As a budding mathematician, logical rules were my specialty.

My parents were both PhD mathematicians. Science and math were the ruling belief systems in our household. Whether it was the weather outside or human evolution, my parents believed inherently in the objectivity of facts—it was their religion.

Naturally, they followed science, as they saw it, in their meticulous approach to dieting. They kept a towering doctor's office scale in the bathroom and updated weight charts on graph paper, noting every pound lost, every pound gained. I had watched this process for years. Now I was joining the effort.

My goal was to lose two pounds a week. That translated into cutting my consumption by one thousand calories per day. For a young nerd like me, this was exciting. Not only was I going to lose weight, I could use my math skills in the process. We had a calorie-counting book on a shelf in the kitchen. I looked up the value of everything I ate in it and then added it all up. By subtracting this sum from my "maintenance amount," I calculated how much more I could eat.

My father explained that if I succeeded in limiting calories I could reward myself at the end of the week with a candy bar of my choice. If I failed, I'd lose my allowance that week. He wielded carrots and sticks to make sure I understood the urgency of the problem.

At first, I loved dieting. Each Saturday, my mom weighed me on our special scale to check on my progress and determine whether I deserved punishment or reward. The scale had two beams, the big one for increments of fifty pounds and the smaller for single pounds. I stepped up, hearing the thud of the scale as it balanced, and watched in anticipation. When I saw that my weight had gone down, the feeling of achievement was intoxicating.

After those first few successes on the scale, I became relentlessly focused on food and my future thin self. I ditched regular meals and instead ate multiple packages of hundred-calorie "fruit snacks," as those made counting calories even easier, and the tiny, bite-sized amounts helped me to slow down my enjoyment. I felt elated, empowered—and totally in control of my body for the first time in my young life.

This dieting honeymoon didn't last. A couple of months into the process, something weird began to happen. I'd start the day strong but by the afternoon I struggled to remember what I'd eaten, or how many calories I'd already consumed. By the end of the day, I'd lost count completely, my precious numbers slipping away from me.

Many readers at this point are no doubt thinking that I was just one more failed dieter, and that I clearly lacked self-control. That is the universal tenet of fat shame: Diets work; dieters fail. And believe me, I embraced this credo as fervently as anyone.

As my lost pounds returned, I began to dread the weekly weigh-ins. Each Saturday, I'd wake up before dawn feeling dark and broken. In hindsight, I know this was shame. But in those early mornings lying awake in bed, I only knew that I was miserable.

I started cheating on the weigh-ins. By taping a triple-A battery, carefully hidden, onto the back of the bottom beam, I managed to hack the scale. This removed a few pounds from the count. The trick worked for a while, but I was terrified of getting caught. And sure enough, after a month or so, my mother, no dummy, started to wonder why after losing so many pounds I looked bigger. She inspected the scale and found the tape I used to mount the battery. I had not only failed as a dieter but also been exposed as a cheater. When she confronted me, I confessed tearfully to my crimes. Shame begot more shame, as it often does.

My mom silently put an end to the diet experiment that day. I started getting my allowance no matter what I weighed. She never explained her reasoning, so I was left to imagine it. What I came up with was this: I was an eleven-year-old nobody, destined to be gross and fat all my life. She'd given up on me.

Throughout this grim drama, as my hopes to transform myself rose and then crashed, I overlooked one stubborn detail: My parents had been dieting, on and off, for years, and *they were still overweight*. They believed devoutly in the apparently scientific grounding of diets. They had tried dozens of them over the years: They counted calories; they tried low fat, low sugar, high bran. (In their desperation, they sometimes strayed from science. My mom briefly experimented with an olive oil diet, which called for a spoonful every time she felt hungry. The idea was to punish yourself for being hungry. A few weeks later I called and asked how it was going but she'd forgotten all about it.) After many promising beginnings, all these diets came to nothing.

I was too young to understand the hypocrisy of two overweight parents pushing their child to succeed where they'd failed. And it certainly didn't occur to me until much later that like me they were ashamed. When I failed in my diet, they pretended it never happened, because my stumbles were shadows of their own.

As I progressed through childhood and adolescence, I continued the effort on my own, trying one diet after another. Each one represented an opportunity to atone for my sins from the previous debacle. Yet every weight-loss program followed the same course: I lost pounds, gained back even more, then moved on to the next magical formula. For decades I trusted that if I was sufficiently worthy, or maybe just lucky, the solution would finally be revealed to me. None worked. The escape routes to normalcy led me right back to where I'd started.

During those years, my shame didn't result from a stand-alone event, like farting in the lunchroom or flunking a history test. It was a chronic condition. I arranged my life, from the clothes I wore to the activities I'd agree to do with friends, to protect myself from shameful episodes, like the weighing scene in the gym, or much later, the confrontation in the bodega. I allowed myself to buy clothes only after I'd dieted successfully for a few weeks, which meant all my clothes were always uncomfortably tight. I kept them that way to punish myself for gaining the weight back. The result was that in addition to being fat, I became chronically uncomfortable and self-punishing.

That's what shame can do. Conditioned to it, we carry its mandates in our minds. In this way, it's as deep within us as our language or religion. Its walls serve their function inside our heads. Fearing to venture beyond its confines, where we might feel the pain of shame, we shrink from opportunities, from fun, from love. That's how shame colonizes our lives.

And it spirals ever downward. Consider the toxic feedback loops. An ashamed hoarder, for example, buffers himself from judgment by inviting no one to his cluttered house. But this leaves him freer to keep acquiring stuff, worsening the problem. And a fat teenager, like me, will naturally shy away from going to the gym, for fear of exposing her body and condition, and the ridicule that might follow. The result is that she falls further out of shape, which makes a visit to the gym ever more hazardous—and less likely. Once people get into this negative shame cycle, a Florida State University study shows, they tend to gain even more weight.

With their health increasingly at risk, fat people get lower-quality medical care, in large part because doctors "can't see past the fat." They blame most heavy patients' symptoms on their weight, shaming them even more and kick-starting a new toxic feedback loop.

Another episode of shame shock that affected me personally involved a doctor who insisted that, because I was so fat, there was no way I could possibly also exercise daily. This was when I was training for a triathlon. And it would have made some sense if I'd come to him for advice about fitness, but I had made the appointment to talk about getting pregnant. It's not hard to see that as much as we inflict shame on ourselves we get a lot of help from others as well.

Because many shamed fat people avoid the medical establishment altogether, they search for quick fixes on late-night TV or the internet. One family member of mine, a very heavy woman, died from complications caused by a crash diet involving dangerous pills. People are literally killing themselves to escape fat shame.

My parents were smart people. In other arenas they assessed evidence and made informed decisions. When my mom was diagnosed with breast cancer, she read all the research papers about her condition and explained the statistics to her doctor. Generally speaking, my parents adjusted their behavior rationally to improve their odds.

However, despite their repeated experience with botched diets, they clung stubbornly to pseudoscientific theories of weight loss. No amount of evidence could steer them away from losing formulas. Shame muddled their thinking and instilled false hopes. Instead of blaming the diets, they blamed themselves—and me.

To our human problem-solving nature, diets just make so much sense. The numbers seem to add up. And they also fit neatly into traditional Western values. If you suffer and endure the hardships of hunger, a thin body is your recompense. Being thin, after all, is viewed as a choice. Having made the right one, which is difficult and requires discipline and righteousness, you can strut your narrow waist size to signal virtue. You can have pride, which in terms of psychic suffering is the polar opposite of shame.

Trouble is, diets rarely "work"—at least when the promise is to transform a fat person into a thin one forever. For most obese people, diets hurt more than they help. After sifting through voluminous records from the final quarter of the twentieth century, UCLA researchers found that between one-third and two-thirds of people who lost weight while dieting did not just regain the pounds in short order. They piled on more. The question for most dieters wasn't whether the lost pounds would return, the researchers wrote, but only how long it would take.

Yet failed formulas have by no means stopped weight loss from growing into a monster $72 billion industry in the United States alone. It doesn't cure the epidemic of obesity but instead grows with it. At last count, the adult obesity rate in the United States was 42.4 percent, and more than one hundred million Americans were on a diet.

The obesity challenge, in fact, is global, and the cause remains a mystery. Even wild animals, by some accounts, are gaining weight. People come up with all kinds of theories, from an atmosphere coursing with endocrine-disrupting chemicals to responses within our cells to perceived threats. These might eventually tell us why so many of the world's creatures are getting fat. Of course, there are endless explanations for humanity's susceptibility: jumbo portions in restaurants, Double Stuf Oreos, too much time slumped on the couch, the ubiquity of fast food, the demise of the family meal, even the decline in smoking. These and countless other factors combine with the stubborn workings of the human body to create the problem, but no one can say exactly how. "Obesity isn't a disease of willpower; it's a biological problem," says Dr. George Bray, a professor at Pennington Biomedical Research Center at Louisiana State University. "Genes load the gun, and environment pulls the trigger."

For shame machines, there is nothing more profitable than a painful and intractable scourge shrouded in mystery. False promises sell, and since they don't work, the market stays strong. Failure, in fact, is central to the dieting business model, fueling earnings for giants like Weight Watchers and Jenny Craig. They profit from a never-ending stream of shame-addled, self-loathing repeat customers. Weight Watchers' former chief financial officer, Richard Samber, told *The Guardian* that 84 percent of the customers failed in their diets and cycled back to the company. "That's where your business comes from," he said.

Weight-loss programs claim remarkable success nonetheless. Their marketing typically features dramatic before-and-after photos with deceiving statistics. It's a textbook case of lying with numbers.

It boils down, as statistics often do, to self-serving choices about what to count. One 2011 study published in *The Lancet*, a prime example of such cherry-picking, found that a group of dieters at Weight Watchers lost twice as much as a control group that had access only to doctors' recommendations. This sounds impressive. The catch? Funded by Weight Watchers, the study covered a period of only twelve months. This is too little time for the dieters to gain back the pounds. According to earlier Weight Watchers research, published in 2008, nearly four of five customers report losing weight in the first year. Yet this success rate plunges to a measly 16 percent after five years.

Darkening the picture even more, the threshold for this so-called success is laughably low. It involves retaining only 5 percent of the weight loss. Say a dieting customer in her early period of triumph drops her weight from 250 to 230 pounds. She poses for the "after" picture, wearing a big smile, and then proceeds to gain back 19 of those 20 pounds. At this point she weighs 249. And yet she has retained 5 percent of her weight loss. Statistically she's a winner, though I'm betting she doesn't feel like one.

In other words, diets that lead to dramatic and lasting weight reduction are statistical outliers. To make their case, diet companies play fast and loose with the word "successful." And the studies they cite are almost always flawed.

Another problem has to do with human nature. We tend to share happy news, while keeping a tight lid on the stuff we're ashamed of. Consider updates on Facebook. You see lots of graduations but not much about students flunking out of school.

The same goes for weight loss. Dieters feel euphoric early in the process, as the pounds melt away. It's an achievement. They're happy to talk. But they tend to clam up when the pounds return. Like me, when I desperately hacked my parents' scale, most people would rather hide their setbacks. Shame muffles their testimony, muddying the statistics. This results in what statisticians call "selection bias." It skews industry data toward success stories, almost all of them short-term. In the 2011 Weight Watchers study, more people dropped out of the Weight Watchers group than the control group. This selection bias is yet another reason to be skeptical of dieting analyses.

Noom, a weight-loss program offering behavior modification, provides a prime example of marketing with sketchy statistics. The company targets upscale dieters, appealing to them in part through sponsorship plugs on National Public Radio. Most of its users are likely aware that diet programs usually fail—they even have a blog post entitled "Why Diets Don't Work"—so the company works this dreary fact into its pitch. "Deep down," it says on its app, "you know this time will be different because you're about to embark on the most modern weight loss course known to man or woman." Noom provides new subscribers with a time chart showing how many months it will take them to reach their target weight. And it assures them that plenty of others following Noom's formula have found success.

This is where the usual statistical games commence. Noom cites its own study claiming that 78 percent of its customers lost weight. Well, I'm glad I'm here to walk us through that research. Please put on your bullshit detectors, everyone.

The analysis included 35,921 participants, all of whom installed the app and recorded their data two or more times a month for six consecutive months. How many other users signed up and never came back, or came back for three or four months—enough time to lose faith in the program? Those people weren't counted. In fact, Noom's decision to track only very active users is guaranteed to weed out people who have been overcome with shame. Selection bias, check.

What's more, Noom rests its case on results gathered over the course of a single year, far too short a time frame. As the 2008 Weight Watchers study demonstrated, dieters who register dramatic weight loss in the first year are all too likely to gain it back in years two through five.

So, once again, while Noom makes money with bad science, let's consider the human toll on the folks who "failed" on the Noom diet. They are made to feel not only fat but condemned to remain so. And it's their fault. Like other toxic forms of shame, this one hinges on a false choice. This failure, as defined by the shame machine, disheartens them every day. It's a lifelong blight. Many promise themselves that in the future they'll work even harder. Next time they won't drop their guard. They'll persist. And they will blame themselves even more intensely when they regain the weight.

———

For businesses, the opportunities to make money from the shame surrounding fat people are boundless. One involves featuring them—the fatter, the better—in a spectacle. This is the premise of *The Biggest Loser* reality show. When the contestants appear on the program, they're very big indeed, chosen to be cartoonishly "in need of help" by the diet industry. And the implicit message to millions of viewers is that they're watching life's losers.

This is a seductive message. Couch potatoes carrying an extra forty or fifty pounds will feel downright svelte, and virtuous, watching these heavy people desperately trying to shed their pounds and their shame. "At least I'm doing better than him," they think. It sounds cruel, and it is. But it's also how we humans who feel shame often buoy ourselves up.

To be honest, I feel that impulse myself. Even while I pen righteous screeds on my blog about how shows like *The Biggest Loser* are profiting from people's shame, I sometimes find myself in that same frame of mind, deflecting shame onto people who appear worse off than I am. Shame isn't a habit you can kick in a day or even a decade. My awareness of it doesn't prevent it from seeping into my thoughts and poisoning my judgments. So I get why the show has a certain crude appeal, not unlike a nineteenth-century circus freak show.

Every weight-loss technique on *The Biggest Loser* is unsustainable. Most are sadistic and perilous for the participants. They volunteer to submit to a near-starvation diet while pushing their bodies every day through hours of frantic exercise under the tutelage of trainers. All of these efforts are minutely tracked by videographers and data analysts.

Rachel Frederickson, the 2014 winner, caused a viral sensation on the internet when she stepped on the scale at the finale and weighed in at a dainty 105 pounds. This was down from 260. She had lost more than half her body weight, and she walked away with $250,000 in prize money.

But once the show ends, those trainers and statisticians are nowhere to be seen. Life resumes its rhythms. Frederickson reported months later that she'd regained twenty pounds. It's hardly surprising. In fact, a study of the contestants from the show's eighth season found that the metabolisms of nearly all the contestants had slowed in the years following the competition. That meant they burned fewer calories at rest. Most of them regained weight, and four of the fourteen studied were heavier six years later than they had been before their televised exhibition.

One person who will never show up on *The Biggest Loser,* much as the show would love to feature her, is the irrepressible singer, rapper, and flutist Lizzo. She's deliciously round and doesn't apologize for it one bit. She whirls and dances as she sings, and shakes her body for the crowd. In one video, she shares Cheetos with friends. Like many, she has gone through periods of body shame, according to interviews. But she seems to have won that battle resoundingly. Lizzo not only accepts herself but loves herself. She urges the audience to do the same, to celebrate life, and to deep-six their fat shame—in short, to be shame-free.

For a weight-loss industry anchored in people's shame and self-loathing, Lizzo poses a threat. So it was no surprise in early 2020 that Jillian Michaels, formerly one of the trainers on *The Biggest Loser,* fat-shamed her. Speaking on BuzzFeed TV, Michaels said, "Why are we celebrating her body?" She added that it "isn't going to be awesome if she gets diabetes." When attacked on social networks for her fat-shaming, Michaels said: "It's not about saying that I don't respect her, or I don't think she's awesome. I absolutely do. But I also would hate to see her get sick."

This kind of shame, where the shamer both denies and defends the tactic, is "concern trolling." It's vicious and condescending, and if you're fat, you face it constantly. People raise health worries and offer advice. Some of them, like the cashier at my Somerville corner store, might think they mean well. But the implication, once again, is that there's a choice. Lizzo has chosen to be fat. She is wrong. She should be ashamed and take it upon herself to mend her ways: She should diet.

This type of concern trolling is based on the assumption that it's never occurred to the fat person to diet, or that they've never tried to before. And of course it's predicated on the false premise that dieters fail only because they lack willpower and discipline (for which, of course, they should be ashamed).

Imagine that Lizzo, instead of being heavy, had epilepsy. In this case, her message to her fans might be that epileptic seizures were nothing to be ashamed of, nor an obstacle to becoming a global star. Would the same chorus of concern trollers urge her to get brain surgery for her condition or take stronger meds? I don't think so, because epilepsy isn't viewed as her "fault." It's not the result of a choice she made. Neither is being fat. Yet it's considered as such. False choices, as we've seen, are the beams and joists that prop up shame.

Lizzo doesn't need protection from concern trollers, because the trolling works only when the target is ashamed. She evidently feels fine about herself. Nonetheless, plenty of people rushed to her defense on social media. A few made excellent points. A writer named Melissa Florer-Bixler noted Lizzo's athleticism and endurance in a since-deleted tweet. "Try running 7 MPH in heels on a treadmill clearly singing the words to Truth Hurts without sounding out of breath," she wrote. "Stop halfway to play the flute for a minute. Now start running again and finish the song. Now do this for two hours . . ."

The main takeaway, though, is not that Lizzo appears to enjoy robust cardio health. It's that she's living her life fully and not letting fat shame weigh her down.

In this respect, at least, she's shame-free, or *shameless*. We usually use that word negatively. A kid peeing into a reservoir, for example, is shameless, because he's unconstrained by society's standards. But when those same norms, and the industries profiting from them, punch down on people, shamelessness can be a healthy and freeing response, even a superpower. In the realm of obesity, a strong dose of shamelessness is the potion we all need.

And that should be the message for kids. When it comes to health, the focus should not be on what's wrong with them or their alleged shortcomings. I know from experience how destructive that can be. Diets can generate a world of hurt for kids, promoting chronic body-image problems, yo-yo dieting, and eating disorders. The alternative would be to focus on enjoying good food, keeping active, and playing.

The effects of childhood diet shaming can stretch on for decades. A 2019 study published in the *Journal of Adolescent Health* concluded that children whose parents urge them to diet often end up with a spouse who performs the same function—and that those people are statistically more likely to struggle with their weight throughout their lives.

Yet that shame-free approach hardly fits the diet industry's business model. Their strategy, increasingly, is to push diet programs for kids. In 2018, the same year that Weight Watchers rebranded itself as WW, the company bought Kurbo Health, an outgrowth of Stanford's Pediatric Weight Loss Program. The following year, WW launched Kurbo, targeting children aged eight to seventeen.

On its website, Kurbo delivers a master class in concern trolling. The company warns that heavy children might face prediabetes, high blood pressure, and other health risks: "Therefore, if your child is overweight, helping him or her get to a healthy weight is one of the best things you can do for them now and in the future."

The kids are furnished with a smartphone app, where they log what they eat. The foods are tagged as green (great), yellow (OK), and red (caution). And they have a video meeting every week with a coach.

I can only imagine how that meeting might feel after back-sliding on a diet. I picture one of Kurbo's customers, perhaps an eleven-year-old girl somewhere, waking up early the morning of her weekly call, filled with anxiety and wishing she could hack the electronic scale or skip the entire process.

Sadly, though, the powerful shame industrial complex has a stake in her unhappiness. It monetizes the false assumptions and phony science that most of us accept and uses them to punch down relentlessly. For that girl, like the rest of us, relief will come only when she manages to free herself from the intergenerational cycles of shame.

CHAPTER 2

SHIFTING THE BLAME

Under a bridge in Daytona Beach, Florida, a mother of three named Blossom Rogers lay in the back seat of her battered minivan and tried to sleep. Blossom had been addicted to crack for nearly two decades. Years earlier, after leaving her three kids with her mother and grandmother, she had followed her addiction. It led her to theft, to prostitution, and to what seemed like an endless cycle of jail and failed rehab. She even spent some time in a mental hospital.

On this warm night in 2004, she listened to the roaring cars and trucks above her. "These people all have lives," she remembers thinking. "And I don't." A few nights later, Blossom sat in a crack house and, between hits on her pipe, she wrote a letter to God, asking for help.

On numerous levels, shame was a constant in her life. Mainstream society, she knew, including all those people crossing the bridge above her, viewed her as contemptible, a lost cause. They had written her off. She was just as hard on herself. She told me she didn't blame the others for the way they saw her because she had such a dismal self-image. Self-loathing, and the secrecy surrounding it, pushed Blossom ever downward and kept her there.

Blossom's story starts in 1966, when she was born to a teenage mother in New Smyrna Beach, Florida. Her father was not around, and Blossom spent her early years with her great-grandmother.

When she was five, her great-grandmother tried to soothe Blossom's ringworm by giving her Colt 45 malt liquor. From that point on, she says she had a drinking problem, among many others. Another of her early memories from that house was of a man opening his fly and telling her to kiss his "worm."

When her mother got married, Blossom moved into the new household. But it was no sanctuary either. Her stepfather abused her sexually, she says, for years. When she threatened to tell her mother, his reply worked every time: "No one will believe you."

"I felt like I had my childhood snatched away from me," she says. And any semblance of it ended when she got pregnant at sixteen. Her plan at the time was to escape from her stepfather by starting a family of her own.

Blossom went on to have rocky relationships with men. After leaving home, she had two more sons before she finally met a man she trusted. He beat her and turned out to be addicted to crack. While he filled her life with suffering, he also offered relief. "I hurt so much inside," she says. "And when I smoked crack, it made me feel like all my pain was gone."

Addiction came to rule her life. She remembers one stormy night pedaling on her bicycle "like the witch in *The Wizard of Oz*," braving thunder and lightning. She wore a plastic bag atop her head as she hunted down "the dopeman."

For the next two decades, she carried her sexual abuse as a dark and shameful secret. "It made me feel like I wasn't worthy." That's a characteristic of chronic shame: It consumes us with doubts about our own worth, leaving us with no energy to fight back against our oppressors.

It's hardly surprising that there would be correlations between shame and addiction. A 2012 study by Australian researchers found that people prone to shame were more likely to engage in problem drinking "as a means of coping." And a 2001 study of women in

Alcoholics Anonymous found that people struggling with addiction who had higher levels of shame were more likely to relapse.

Yet many recovery programs are anchored in shame, blaming people for their addictions, even as studies warn that such an approach is counterproductive. Psychology researchers at UCLA divided seventy-seven cigarette smokers into two groups and gave each participant eight cigarettes, a lighter, and an ashtray. They were offered monetary awards for resisting the temptation during the hour they were left alone.

One of these groups, however, was exposed to negative stereotypes collected from anti-smoking campaigns. They were subjected to explicit shame that questioned their willpower and dedication to health.

The group exposed to the stigmatizing messages lit up earlier. Seventy percent of them started smoking within twenty minutes compared to 40 percent of the control group. The researchers theorize that the smokers were responding to so-called stereotype threat. When this happens, people's worries and fears overwhelm their minds—deflecting their efforts to counteract the stereotypes.

Yet shame doesn't work alone. Peer pressure, boredom, and desperation all play a part in addictive behaviors, as do a host of biological signals, many still wrapped in mystery. For Blossom Rogers, there was also the allure of fun. "I liked everything about crack cocaine," she recalls. "The fast life, the orgies. But I didn't like the consequences."

She was a woman in dire need of help and compassion. Yet society heaped ever more shame upon her, along with hundreds of thousands of other people addicted to crack. The epidemic, which exploded in inner cities in the 1980s, provides a textbook case of victimizing the afflicted. Society punched down with a vengeance, unleashing toxic cycles of shame. In stark contrast to the shaming clowns we saw in Pueblo cultures, who nudged community members back toward shared values and inclusion, the shame cascading over people with a crack addiction only worsened the scourge. It destroyed lives, families, and entire communities.

The crack tragedy began with a marketing scheme of evil genius, one that would make for an excellent business school case study. Faced with a glut of cocaine and collapsing prices, traffickers in the early 1980s dramatically expanded their market by creating a cheap and smokable form of the drug that just happened to be highly addictive, further enhancing their business strategy.

Hundreds of thousands of people became hooked on crack as it swept through American cities and unleashed mass panic. According to lurid reports in the newspapers and on TV, crack made them crazed and highly dangerous. Gun violence was rampant. Addicted Black women gave birth to so-called crack babies who apparently faced torturous withdrawals.

Like other shame machines, the one about crack babies was grounded in dubious science. Reports accepted as gospel by many politicians and newspapers predicted that traces of cocaine would overstimulate the fetal brain, resulting later in hyperaggressiveness, manic depression, and attention deficit disorder. John Silber, then the president of Boston University, went further. He warned that crack babies would grow up with minds so stunted that they would never achieve "consciousness of God." The columnist Charles Krauthammer wrote, "Theirs will be a life of certain suffering, of probable deviance, of permanent inferiority."

This unsubstantiated so-called science fit the narrative of failure and aberration, and it pushed the shame into punishing overdrive. In the summer of 1989, a twenty-three-year-old named Jennifer Clarice Johnson gave birth to a baby and was promptly charged in Florida with distributing drugs to an underage child. Because the law didn't apply to fetuses, prosecutors focused on the sixty seconds after the birth, before the umbilical cord was severed. Johnson was found guilty, an appeal was upheld, and the young mother was sentenced to fourteen years of probation, along with rehab.

It was reasonable, of course, to be concerned about the effects of drugs on fetuses. But much of the analysis was based on loose associations. The damage that fetal alcohol syndrome could inflict on a developing brain was well documented. So it stood to reason, in the eyes of many, that a dangerous and addictive drug like crack would be even worse. Plus it seemed right that these people who in society's view had made bad choices would be suffering the consequences.

But the dire predictions concerning the brain development of crack babies turned out to be false. Many of these children, to be sure, faced great challenges, from poverty to parents struggling with addiction. But crack, unlike alcohol, didn't alter their brains.

The epidemic had a face and, in the popular mind, it was Black. And it had a geography, the mean streets of American cities. These were the neighborhoods middle-class Americans rarely ventured into, and if by chance they did, they'd lock the car doors and shut the windows, many resolving never to stop, not even to fix a flat tire. In short, these neighborhoods ravaged by the epidemic seemed to be hell on earth.

Who was responsible for this infernal mess? In the mind of the shaming public, it came down, once again, to people making bad choices. When offered a pipe and a lighter, Blossom should have said no. Instead she said yes. Thus she, and others like her, were responsible for their problems and should be ashamed of themselves. People addicted to crack had flouted society's rules. They clearly didn't have the values or the grit to succeed.

That was the view of the ruling class, the policymakers, the business leaders, and in fact most Americans who were doing OK. Their kids, after all, were making the right choices. Instead

of sitting on street corners, taking drugs, and sticking up convenience stores, they were playing varsity sports or practicing violin.
Yes, maybe they zoned out too much on videogames or goofed off
at school. And, sure, many experimented with drugs and drank.
But as a population, they were moving in the right direction. Those
headed for the brightest futures were studying for college entrance
exams and padding their résumés with all sorts of extracurricular
activities.

In other words, the response to the crack epidemic, in most
of the country, was to blame the victims. This meant taking only
minimal measures to help afflicted communities confront this
terrifying public health crisis. Instead, legislators imposed draco-
nian punishments and attempted to distance themselves from the
problem. Hundreds of thousands, including enormous numbers of
young Black males, were sent to prison for crack-related offenses,
many facing obscenely long sentences.

Crack, it was believed back then, was a far more frightening
drug than cocaine, its more expensive chemical cousin. Crack made
people violent. It was more addictive. While cocaine was a scourge,
crack was a raging wildfire. Yet there was another issue, mostly
unspoken: The people who made laws were familiar with cocaine.
They knew it from college dorms and parties; a good number of
them had snorted a few lines. Crack, in their eyes, was a "ghetto"
drug. They associated it with other people.

At the height of the crack epidemic, this distinction was
encoded into racist federal law. The so-called 100-to-1 rule, passed
in 1986, stipulated a sentence of no less than five years for carrying
five hundred grams of cocaine, or a bit more than a pound. But
those carrying a mere five grams of crack, just a few pebbles, faced
the same minimum. In other words, an investment banker caught
in the bathroom with a quarter pound of cocaine, worth perhaps

$25,000, could often avoid jail time. Inner-city kids with a $15 vial of crack, on the other hand, were locked up for at least five years.

Urban neighborhoods, already staggering under the epidemic, saw their young sent away. They were powerless, buried under many layers of state-sponsored punishment and shame. For starters, the term for the victims was "addict." This wasn't a state they were in, like unemployed, or a disease they suffered from, like cancer or depression. It was a noun. "Addict" defined what they were and was nearly synonymous with "wrong choice." The word reflected their faulty morals and wayward path through life.

Young Black men, especially, were also shamed for getting into trouble and abandoning their families. But locking up hundreds of thousands of them only made it worse. It branded them. In addition to being poor, Black, and addicted, they now bore the stigma of felon, which virtually eliminated legal employment opportunities. And when many returned to the only business they knew and got caught again, they were sent away for even longer sentences. In some states, Three Strikes, You're Out statutes put them behind bars forever. Society didn't want to invest in these lives and preferred instead to bury them.

In this sense, stigma results in shame, because it signals who is valued and who is not in the eyes of society. When institutions and governments assign themselves stigmatizing roles, they create systems of assigned merit. In other words, if you are told by all the world that you are not worthy, you often end up feeling that way. The result: The crack epidemic unleashed a frenzy of punching-down shame.

What was the alternative? Consider Blossom trying to sleep under the Florida bridge. If she were your sister or your daughter, what would you suggest? The first step, no doubt, would be to help her beat her addiction. Rehab would work best if she had a safe place to live, ideally surrounded by a supportive community, perhaps including her children. Job training would prepare her for the future.

This path, however, requires empathy. It means looking at the victims not as losers or outcasts but as family members—even if only part of our human family—who need help.

Empathy, though, is hard work, especially when it involves people we don't know. In this case, it was much easier for society to shame the victims and relegate them to the realm of *other*—folks with alien values who make stupid and disastrous choices. That's what made the racist policies so appealing: It was another way of "othering" the people with an addiction. The default option was to keep a safe emotional distance and let them marinate in their own mess.

Typical of this mindset is a 1989 op-ed in *The Boston Globe*. Written by a doctor in a Washington, D.C., hospital, it describes the mothers of babies born with crack-cocaine dependencies: "These women live in filth." Their addictions represented "a totally selfish response. . . . There's not much that they care about." In this view, prevalent in America at the time, those addicted to crack inhabited a far-off and amoral universe.

Empathy requires time and attention. Even well-meaning people are busy. Those outside the neighborhoods devastated by drugs and associated crime had jobs to worry about, kids to raise, bills to pay. For the great majority of them, freeing up more time to care about people addicted to drugs was a nonstarter. And since the victims were physically removed from the American mainstream, cloistered in their ravaged neighborhoods, it was much easier to ignore them.

Then there's money. Rehab programs were expensive, and so were living quarters, food, and continued therapy. Prison, of course, cost even more—about $30,000 per year, a decent middle-class salary at the time, in federal lockups. (And the outsourcing of prison management to private companies yields cash flow and profits, and revenue of more than $3 billion per year in 2018.) However, to the shaming public, prison felt appropriate in spite of the financial burden. It gave the drug offenders the punishment they deserved, while therapy and halfway houses would only coddle them and provide services for free.

If we look hard enough, we can find examples of people who break out of addiction. And their stories—like those of the rare successful dieters—sustain our shaming narratives.

This brings us back to Blossom Rogers. In interviews on Christian programs and in the three books she has written, she gives thanks to God for her recovery. And it is true that faith, along with the backing of a religious community, can provide valuable support to people struggling with addiction.

Yet the impression left by her story reinforces the myths that sustain the poisonous punching-down status quo. It would seem that a woman who had made a long series of poor choices—opting for pregnancies, drugs, abusive friends and lovers—found a way to turn the corner. Through the strength of her will and her faith she swung from the wrong decisions to the right ones. If only more people would follow her path to salvation!

Blossom is a survivor. She's a remarkable person with a special spirit. However, inspiring stories like Blossom's are the exception, not the rule, and that's the point. Otherwise, they wouldn't be noteworthy. They also fit our agenda. If Blossom manages to reclaim her life, the thinking goes, others can too. It's up to them. No need for us to empathize, much less help them. In fact, we can continue to punch down on them mercilessly, feeling righteous in our choices while shaming them for theirs. We can consign them to the slums and jails we never see. And when they're ready to change their shameful ways, well, they're on their own.

The other crucial detail about Blossom's story is that in addition to her faith and inner strength, she benefited from effective rehab. After checking into a mental hospital, where she stayed for three days, she was sent to a transitional rehab house, which provided counseling, as well as a safe and drug-free place to live.

This raises an important caveat. An undersized contingent of people in churches, hospitals, and clinics do battle against the addiction shame machine, working hard on behalf of the victims. Such institutions are miserably underfunded, but they have their successes. Blossom Rogers is one. I've known others.

In the spring of my sophomore year of high school, I was in a very bad way, severely depressed and at risk of suicide. I landed in Emerson Hospital near my home in Lexington. My roommate was anorexic, but most of my fellow patients were victims of the drug epidemic raging in scary neighborhoods I'd only heard about, never seen. Some were addicted to heroin. A few abused cocaine. But most of them were addicted to crack. After all, this was 1987.

If I hadn't been so screwed up myself, I never would have met these people, much less connected with them. But a funny and beautiful thing can take place in the psychiatric ward of a hospital. Our mutual shame turned out to be a great equalizer. All of us were seriously disturbed in one way or another. From society's vantage point, we had made bad decisions. But since we were all in the same boat, there was no need to dwell on our shame. We could unpack our lives free of judgment. It was a refuge from the shame machine.

In group therapy, every voice was welcome and empathy abounded. I told long-buried stories—about my childhood, my family, my shame caused by sexual abuse. Some of them had never even passed through my conscious mind. And I heard others' harrowing accounts of childhood abuse and suffering, of addictions and betrayals, which were far more extreme than my stories. I came to see my fellow patients not as criminals or failures but as refugees from psychological war zones.

Within this group, people weren't monitoring my weight, scrutinizing my every pound, as I had learned to do from my parents. They weren't competing with me for grades or casting me out as a weirdo, as they did in my high school. With them, I was just me. It was the first time in my life that I realized there was a world beyond my house and school—a world where people would take me as I was. With them, for the first time ever, I felt forgivable.

These days, a white girl from the cushy suburbs doesn't have to check into a mental hospital to find common ground with people addicted to drugs. Victims are no longer as hidden from the rest of us. While the crack epidemic was largely confined to the nation's cities, the twenty-first-century opioid crisis spills across the map, into suburbs and rural towns. It's a more equal-opportunity scourge.

But even without the redlining of the crack crisis, we create borders in our minds. We tend to separate victim populations, shaming some of them and sparing others the harshest judgments. War veterans who got hooked on opioids while managing pain, we might say, should not be placed in the same shame-drenched cohort as individuals nodding off on San Francisco's needle-littered Market Street after shooting heroin. The first group is innocent, the second guilty.

Yet these distinctions turn out to be illusory. Some of those people using heroin in San Francisco could well be war veterans. Others could be former members of Congress, heads of hedge funds, suburban mothers. Whatever triggered each person's addiction is by now history, and the evil they're grappling with is a life-threatening disease. In their desperation, people struggling with addiction jump from one fix to another—from OxyContin to heroin to fentanyl—whatever's at hand to ease the torture of withdrawal. So the chemical makeup of one person's addiction hinges less on taste, values, or culture than on supply chains, whether originating in pharma labs or the poppy fields of Mexico. The choice of drug is largely a function of economics, chiefly price and availability.

The addictions these drugs create are accompanied by deep shame, which prevents the afflicted from seeking the assistance they need. Society, fixated on the victims' aberrant behavior, largely withholds this help—both the therapy and substitute medication. Instead, it marches them off by the thousands to prison. Publicly traded corporations, from pharma giants to private prisons, profit from this grim status quo and perpetuate their thriving empires by casting blame on the victims and shaming them into subscribing to their offerings. Bogus rehab outfits turn the tragedy into cruel farce through so-called work therapy, which in some places amounts to indentured servitude. All of this deepens the shame cycle, which nourishes these cruel industries. The more shame in their target market, the richer the returns.

But only up to a point. In a sense, the vendors of addictive drugs, whether heroin or OxyContin, thrive on our illnesses. In this, they're much like the populations of protozoa that inhabit our bodies. Plasmodium, for example, free rides on the *Anopheles* mosquito and infects its victims with malaria. These protozoa, like parasitic manufacturers of addictive painkillers, flourish as the host bodies suffer. But they navigate a delicate balance. If the host dies, that source of livelihood vanishes.

This brings me, sadly, to the story of Jeff Pleus. The experience of Jeff, a white college graduate in Binghamton, New York, shows the differences—from cultural diversity to geographic span—between the opioid epidemic and the crack epidemic.

But it also shows how much hasn't changed. Like victims of the crack crisis, including Blossom, Jeff suffered under layer upon layer of shame. This silenced and punished him, while creating new corporate revenue streams.

In high school, Jeff got solid grades. Like many of his classmates, he dabbled in drugs, smoked a bit of pot. He told his mother, Alexis, that he'd tried cocaine a few times. Universities are full of such people, and many go on to successful careers. Unlike Blossom at the same point in her life, when she was victimized by deprivation and sexual abuse, Jeff had little reason to feel shame.

When Jeff was a junior in high school, in 2003, he had knee surgery. The doctor prescribed OxyContin to kill the pain. This opioid had been launched with much fanfare only seven years earlier by Purdue Pharma, of Hartford, Connecticut. In yet another example of the phony science surrounding addiction, Purdue marketed the drug as a safe and nonaddictive pain-killing alternative. It was a controlled-release pill, engineered to work around the clock. And Purdue's hyperaggressive national salespeople, all of them chasing fat bonuses for meeting sales targets, polished and repeated this lie as they sold Oxy to doctors and hospitals across America.

Jeff's mother told me that at the time she was unaware of the risks. She recalls prodding her son to take the drug. "Have you taken the pill for your pain?" she would ask.

One day, riding in the car, Jeff said to her, "Mom, I think I'm starting to like those pain pills a little too much."

"You'd better quit then," she said.

What she didn't understand, she now realizes, is that Jeff was calling for help. Like most of us, Alexis had been socialized to view addiction as a choice: If her son felt the threat of addiction, and he clearly did, he would make the correct decision. He would avoid trouble. But by that point, Jeff's addiction was beyond his control, growing more serious by the day. As his dependency grew, so did his shame. Naturally, he followed shame's central mandate and cloaked his addiction.

He had reason to. People with a substance use disorder, after all, were widely deemed losers. And Purdue, the manufacturer of the addictive drug, made sure to reinforce this stigma.

Across the country, the opioid epidemic was spreading. It would kill some four hundred thousand in the United States over the following two decades, and the public, from health officials to plaintiff's attorneys, was starting to raise questions about OxyContin's role in the crisis. The company's strategy was to blame the victims. In a 2001 internal email, Richard Sackler, the chairman and former president of the firm, wrote: "We have to hammer on the abusers in every way possible. They are the culprits and the problem. They are reckless criminals."

In this unforgiving environment, people like Jeff worked hard to disguise their addiction. He graduated from Windsor Central High School and then the State University of New York at Morrisville. He went on to get a job. As far as his mother was concerned, her son was launched. His knee surgery and the painkillers he'd taken were a distant memory to her.

Then one day in 2011, out of the blue, she got a phone call from the police. Jeff had been arrested for burglary. Alexis was shocked. Her son had never been a bad kid. When she talked to him on the phone, he insisted that he was innocent, and she believed him. But while Alexis was puzzling over her son's case with a public defender, she heard him say, "A lot of things heroin addicts do don't make sense."

"It was like a punch in the gut," Alexis told me. When she confronted her son, he burst into tears and said, "I'm so sorry, Mom. I'm so ashamed. I'm so embarrassed. I needed help. I need help. But I didn't dare tell you because I was so ashamed."

At this point, you might think that Jeff would be headed for recovery. After all, he had told his mother the truth and broken free of the shame cycle. Now he could stop hiding. With the support of a loving family, he could battle his addiction in rehab. But he encountered a society much more willing to send people with an addiction to prison than to effective rehab. "We had excellent insurance," Alexis says, "top-of-the-line." And yet when she managed to get Jeff out of jail, after five weeks, and started calling rehab facilities, she learned that since he had been off drugs since his arrest, and was no longer actively using them, he did not qualify for treatment.

Society's response to Jeff's opioid addiction was, in effect, to dismiss him. The message was to quit or, as First Lady Nancy Reagan repeated throughout the 1980s, "just say no." To much of the public this sounded like the simplest advice. But to people suffering from addiction, it was insulting and shaming. It once again framed addiction as a choice, and the clear yet unspoken judgment was that those who failed to "just say no" were guilty of making foolish and calamitous decisions. Society could forget about them. Their downfall was their own doing.

Of course, a strategy that offered a lot of shame and little real help utterly failed. And most of the victims were condemned to fall by the wayside, either by wasting away in prison or by overdosing.

By far the most effective therapy for opioid addiction provides behavioral counseling for the patient along with substitute drugs, such as methadone and buprenorphine. While there are no medicines to ease people addicted to crack from their dependency, replacement drugs offer a lifeline to those addicted to opioids. Known as Medication-Assisted Treatment (MAT), it "significantly reduces illicit opioid use compared with non-drug approaches," according to a 2016 study by the Pew Charitable Trusts. Increased access to these therapies can cut back on overdose fatalities as well as associated risks, including HIV, hepatitis C, and street violence.

Advocates for victims of addiction, however, struggle to sell MAT to a skeptical public. One reason is that the therapy accepts addiction as a disease, one to be managed with medicine, and not as a wrong and shameful choice. MAT focuses on reclaiming people's lives and relationships and freeing them from reliance on dangerous drugs that lead them into crime and can kill them. But MAT, at least in its early phases, does not vanquish the evil. Instead, it replaces one dependency for another.

This does not satisfy a public ethos defined by shame. It seems to indulge people with addictions, instead of pressing them to change their ways. What's more, MAT costs a lot.

The government, to its credit, has advocated more therapy. Both the second Bush and Obama administrations pushed through regulations forcing health insurers to reimburse for some rehab treatments. However, they failed to establish firm standards and best practices. The result is a rich flow of revenue, which feeds a vast, wild, and largely unregulated rehab market.

It's a $35 billion industry rife with scam artists, glib promises, and phony science. What's more, it's based on the false premise that a week or a month in rehab—however it's delivered—will fix the patient. Yet rehab is not like a hip replacement or a tonsillectomy. It takes time. There are setbacks. Therapies that treat addiction as something that can be cured in a month generally lead to relapses and recidivism. So those with addictions, like Blossom and Jeff, cycle through brief rehab stints, the streets, and jail, many of them never fully recovering. Society views them as losers. And as they accept this verdict, their shame deepens.

Why don't we spend the necessary money to treat addiction as a chronic disease? Because it's easier and cheaper to shame the people with drug and alcohol problems and wash our hands of them. Compare, for example, someone addicted to opioids with another suffering from kidney failure. Health insurance pays handsomely to sustain kidney patients not for a month or two but for as long as they need treatment. The government, through Medicare, mandates it. Dialysis is a multibillion-dollar industry. It's also an economic pillar in cities like Denver, where DaVita, Inc., the industry titan, has its headquarters.

In a very real sense, though, a dialysis session is like a dose of methadone. Both therapies distance patients from the ravages of their disease and sustain them until they need treatment again.

Now imagine if people viewed malfunctioning kidneys as shameful, and if governments and insurers, interpreting the national mood, pinched pennies on funding for dialysis. In such a scenario, kidney patients would be on a never-ending hunt for both dialysis and the money to pay for it. With kidneys failing and pain overwhelming their bodies, some would grow frantic. In their desperation, they might hold up convenience stores or snatch purses.

Such is the agonizing existence of a person with an addiction. And in most cases, we continue as a society to punch down on them. For many, the default treatment centers are jails and prisons, whose costs far exceed those of the more humane MAT. But locking people up provides a simple, if heartless, solution: It gets them off the streets and out of sight. According to the National Sheriffs' Association, two-thirds of the jailed population is struggling with drug abuse or addiction.

Some jails and prisons attempt to treat inmates with medicine and provide counseling. However, they're woefully unprepared for this work, both in budget and in expertise. In Middlesex County, a hard-hit area north of Boston, Sheriff Peter Koutoujian estimates that his jail has to provide 40 percent of new inmates with MAT, while at least four-fifths of the prison population battles drug or alcohol dependency.

Since our penal code is not designed for addiction rehabilitation, prisoners are released when their time is up, regardless of the status of their recovery. Once sprung, they find very little in the way of support or halfway houses. They're just back on the streets, usually hanging with the same crowd as before. Many of them are still addicted. Tragically, the forced abstinence in jail lowers their resistance. So in their first days of freedom, startling numbers of them overdose. Talk about a throwaway population.

Jeff Pleus seemed trapped in the netherworld of addiction. After his initial jailing, his attempts to break free of his addiction were short-lived. His girlfriend was also on drugs. For two years, the couple bounced around, losing apartments and jobs, spending a few days in treatment centers, never able to stay sober for long. There were arrests. They'd say to Alexis, "We just want help. Can't you get us help?"

Alexis finally found what she thought was a month of treatment for Jeff through the family insurance, and a shorter one, through a government agency, for his girlfriend. After eleven days at the facility, Alexis recalls, Jeff phoned her. "He was crying, saying he was being sent home because insurance wouldn't pay for more."

Not long after that, he was arrested and spent ten months in jail. He was out and sober for another ten months. But when he used again, his tolerance was virtually gone, making him vulnerable to overdose. By age twenty-eight, he was dead.

Even as our governments scrimp on rehab, it still represents a lucrative profit engine. The industry ranges from so-called clean houses, some of them operated by people with an addiction, to spa-like recovery centers costing tens of thousands of dollars per month. One of them, Cliffside Malibu in California, collects $73,000 a month for a single room and offers everything from yoga to horse petting (billed as "equine therapy").

Others are scandalously cheap—even free—the catch being that the patients earn their keep by working for no pay. Jennifer Warren ran one of them. Once addicted to crack herself, she said she had been cured at a rehab unit in Alabama that featured work therapy, and she was inspired to start her own facility. According to a 2018 investigation by *Reveal*, Warren cofounded Recovery Ventures in 2002 in both Raleigh and Winston-Salem, North Carolina. She got into trouble with the state licensing board for ethical breaches, such as exploiting clients. But after getting fired in 2011, she simply launched another rehab company, Recovery Connections, and continued with the same free-labor business model, this time as caregivers for the elderly and disabled.

Judges would order emotionally vulnerable, addicted people to "do time" at Recovery Connections. Some forty rehabbers there worked for free, *Reveal*'s research showed, some as janitors and cooks. But most of them cared for the elderly. This involved hoisting them into baths, changing diapers, and sometimes even administering the very medicines that they were addicted to. Workdays stretched to eighteen hours, and all of them without pay. These people were reduced to indentured servitude or, as some might have it, slavery.

If that wasn't enough, Recovery Connections also prescribed a sadistic therapy known as Synanon. Developed in the 1950s, its goal is to break people down and supposedly strip away their defenses. So after long days of work, patients would treat one another as punching bags for shame. They would gather in circles around one unfortunate (and no doubt miserable) target. And for forty-five minutes, they would scream insults: spoiled brat, stupid bitch, motherfucking whore.

Amazingly, despite lawsuits from former customers and exhaustively reported journalistic exposés, Recovery Connections still seems to be in business. State authorities visit once a year, and judges continue to send people recovering from addiction there. And it's not the only rehab that puts its patients to work.

This is a business model that thrives on shame. And its vulnerable population recovering from addiction is highly unlikely to rise up and rebel. From the company's perspective, their clients' shame serves as a muzzle. This scheme seems to work for both government agencies and insurers: Because it costs a lot less than other rehabs, it's a budget-friendly option for judges. (They certainly aren't about to send folks on a $73,000 sojourn to Cliffside Malibu.)

Both types of rehab, the indentured servitude in North Carolina and the pampering spa in California, operate in an industry where anything goes. Science is optional; the sky-high success rates printed on their promotional materials are unverified. Make the clients pet horses, dance, or carry a nonagenarian from the toilet to bed. And if the therapy fails and the same patient returns a second or third time? The cash continues to flow. What's wrong with customer loyalty?

Such an industry only exists, and grows, because we choose to punch down on people struggling with addiction. Yes, their lives are precious to their families and friends. But as a society, we don't give a damn. Out of sight, out of mind. They should be ashamed of themselves, we coldly conclude. So they can fix themselves—or not.

CHAPTER 3

THE UNDESERVING POOR

Scott Hutchins is homeless in New York City and has been shuttled from one shelter to the next since 2012. That was when he had a run of bad luck, including a job that fell through in Florida and a slipped disc that left him physically hurting, and with no lease and all of his stuff in storage. The way he tells it, the welfare and shelter systems seem designed to make people feel miserable about themselves. When he was first homeless, he was sent to the Bellevue shelter in lower Manhattan, a place that he says looks like a prison. After two weeks there, they woke him up in the middle of the night and told him to put all of his stuff in a garbage bag. He was getting transferred to another shelter in Brooklyn.

When the COVID-19 crisis hit in 2020, they moved Hutchins and lots of other homeless people again—this time into hotels, two to a room. But they were careful first to remove the cushy beds and replace them with uncomfortable cots. "They want it to be difficult," he says. "They want to shame you."

So far, we've seen an abundance of moneymaking opportunities within the industrial shame complex: weight-loss consultancies, pharmaceutical giants, addiction camps—they all build rich markets and prey upon their customers.

Poor people, by definition, aren't swimming in cash, but there are work-arounds. Loan sharks and bogus for-profit universities fleece the poor by coaxing them to borrow money, driving millions of them deeper into disastrous debt. State governments milk them with one-in-a-million lotteries. Slumlords and subprime auto lenders thrive at their expense. There is money to be made, and desperate people are the easiest marks.

Much of the punching down, though, is focused less on squeezing money from people like Scott Hutchins than on keeping it in the hands of the rich. The poor, in this view, represent a cost. And the voting and tax-paying public is eager to minimize such outlays. The government represents this view, and politicians of both parties have been nurturing it, especially since the 1980s. The crux of their punching-down message: However little you're getting, it's more than you *deserve*.

This righteous attitude confronts an outstretched hand with a fist. Shaming the poor not only saves the wealthier classes money but also makes them feel virtuous. It's akin to the self-satisfaction felt by the thin in the presence of the obese and the sober when comparing themselves to those with a drug or alcohol problem. We succeeded, they think. These others failed. It is this mindset, once again, that sustains the shamescape.

So not only are poor people condemned to live in dangerous neighborhoods with bad schools and dirty air, scrounging for food, shelter, and transportation, but they must also endure wave upon wave of society's shame pouring down on them from above. And if we've made them feel too ashamed to ask for help, the thinking goes, so much the better. Maybe it will change their behavior.

Much of public policy in America embodies the judgment that people are poor because they're lazy. Yet even politicians who blame the poor for their plight are aware of what appear to be exceptions. These form a subgroup of the needy, the so-called *deserving* poor. They include people who can prove they have tried to work but have suffered a few bad breaks. They are worthy of our help.

Perversely, the gatekeepers of privilege seem so hooked on a certain narrative of the deserving poor that they often demand it. This is especially prevalent in higher education. When I visited a class of Black and Brown high school students in Brooklyn, they detailed how the college admissions process forces them to wallow in shame. The colleges and universities, as they see it, demand a certain narrative for disadvantaged students: a story of overcoming the odds and climbing from dreadful and dangerous circumstances, the worse the better. This places them among the deserving. "So I'm supposed to write about the most terrible thing that happened in my life," says one student who was applying for a grant. "A heart-wrenching essay. What if I tell you about how happy I was? I'm not going to be getting money."

This "deserving" contingent of the poor grew explosively in 2020 with the economic devastation brought on by the COVID-19 pandemic. And yet, rather than expanding our empathy, the crisis exposed the same poisonous dichotomy between deserving and undeserving. Even warmhearted politicians and television journalists advocating for those in need contributed to the divide. Their common refrain was that the recent wave of victims found themselves at loose ends "through no fault of their own." Still, the millions who had lost their jobs found themselves confronting overburdened bureaucracies whose governing mandate was to treat everyone applying for benefits as a potential fraudster, and to minimize outlays.

Ronald Reagan excelled at creating a narrative that shamed victims. Running against Gerald Ford in 1976 for the Republican presidential nomination, Reagan regaled crowds with tales of women who gamed the welfare system by having more babies. These were "welfare queens." They raked in enough to drive Cadillacs and eat at fancy restaurants—all while many of his supporters struggled paycheck to paycheck. It was an us-versus-them narrative:

honest, hardworking Americans on one side, welfare cheats on the other.

Reagan based his stories on articles published by *Reader's Digest* and *Look* magazine. These cherry-picked examples came to stigmatize an entire swath of U.S. society, African Americans living in cities. The men, according to this narrative, abandoned their families for drugs and other crime, while single mothers cheated the welfare system. The conclusion was both simple and wonderfully convenient for a tax-cutting movement: The poverty of the urban poor belonged to them. It was their own *choice*. Women, in this view, were freeloaders who chose to have children out of wedlock in order to cash welfare checks. Government largess would only perpetuate the rotten status quo.

It was easy for Reagan and others to defame the urban poor, because the welfare-queen stories seemed to confirm long-standing prejudices. (A similar phenomenon is occurring in the twenty-first century, with the scapegoating of immigrants.) The challenge for policymakers, though, was to sift the poor into two piles: the deserving and the undeserving.

Here they could count on some support from large sectors of the poor themselves. This is due to what social researchers call "last-place aversion." Poverty, in much of the world, is so tainted by shame that people who are poor go to great lengths not to associate themselves with it, and to contrast their position, favorably, with those who are even poorer. This undermines solidarity among the poor and helps draw the fault line between the supposedly deserving and undeserving.

One tactic lawmakers used to separate the two cohorts was to establish work requirements. In many states, the poor have to work, or at least demonstrate that they are applying for employment on a regular basis, to qualify for certain benefits. This punches down especially hard on the urban poor. Take, for example, a single mother in downtown Detroit, Houston, or Los Angeles. The only apartment she can afford is likely to be in a transit desert with scant employment opportunities nearby. Riding a bus to and from a minimum wage job might take hours each day. And that's assuming she has a relative around to care for her children, because the government provides no help there. She's condemned to failure and punished for it.

This bleak status quo is sustained by racist myths and misleading statistics. First of all, in the 1970s, when the welfare-queen trope was popularized, African Americans accounted for only 35 percent of welfare recipients. Yet they were convenient to demonize—and to shame.

To economize on benefits, the government continues to wield numbers from a bygone era. The threshold of poverty, established by the Census Bureau in the middle of the last century, is laughably obsolete. It assumes that poor families will feature a working father and his wife, "a careful shopper," who prepares the family meals. It estimates that her spending on food will represent fully one-third of the family budget. This calculation puts the poverty line for a family of four, in 2018, at $2,100 per month. That's barely enough for rent in many American cities. And this goes a long way toward explaining why a staggering 1.5 million school-age children in the United States were homeless during at least part of the 2017–18 academic year. That's a horrifying statistic, and worse when you consider that this homelessness epidemic expanded during a period of economic boom.

Statisticians choose what they count. That's axiomatic. State and local governments in the United States often configure the poverty line to undercount expenses like rent, food, and healthcare costs. This saves taxpayer money, at least in the short term, and punishes the working poor. If you set the threshold, for example, at $2,100 for a family of four, a struggling Uber driver who works crazy hours to make $2,200 per month counts as someone who has pulled himself up from poverty, even while he may be homeless or drowning in credit card debt. But the biggest shortcoming of poverty statistics is that they reduce the experience to numbers and ignore the human pain and despair of being poor. Those factors resist measurement but are fundamental to the equation.

The Vietnam War provides a case study in the consequences of flawed metrics. Throughout the bloodiest years of the American involvement, from 1964 to 1969, the Pentagon provided daily "body counts" of enemy soldiers. These numbers, repeated every evening by news anchors, gave the impression that the Americans and their allies were making progress, and winning the war. What the numbers missed, though, was psychology: the determination of the Vietnamese, and the spreading hopelessness among the Americans, the growing sense that their enemies, fighting on their home turf, would eventually prevail. These dark forebodings could not be quantified. But for anyone who wanted to understand the status of the war and its likely outcome, they were essential.

In America, poor people have minimal power. Submerged in institutional shame, they lose again and again. They're told ad nauseam that they've screwed up and made disastrous choices. And that conclusion is widely held. So who in American society would want to march under the banner of "poor"?

Many of the people who qualify for government assistance don't even sign up for it. The application ordeal is often pitiless and demeaning. People have to document their lowly material status, their slips, stumbles, disappointments, and humiliations. And the benefits they receive often stigmatize them. One of the most painful memories of his life, writes Issac Bailey, a journalist in South Carolina, came when his mother sent him to the local supermarket, a grocery list in one hand, food stamps in the other. He still recalls the withering looks from fellow shoppers and the checkout clerk. "Little else I have done in the intervening three decades of life," he writes, "made me feel as much shame as I did that day."

For many, the shame of poverty can feel worse than material suffering. Yet while dollars can be tallied on budgets and Excel spreadsheets, feelings cannot. They're intangible and subjective. So we often discount them. This helps turn policies into shaming engines.

Take school lunch. Many school districts across the country struggle to get parents to pay for their child's meal. A common tactic, when a student's lunch account is running a deficit, is to shame the child. In one Pennsylvania school, a seventh-grade girl, whom we will call Chelsea to protect her from further scrutiny, was in line in the cafeteria, getting her slice of pizza, apple, chopped cucumber, and a glass of chocolate milk. But the cafeteria employee saw that the girl had an unpaid bill and threw the food in the trash.

It's a perfect example of poverty shaming: a searing embarrassment that Chelsea (and her classmates) will no doubt carry through high school and beyond. Worse, the child had no responsibility for her unpaid lunch bill; she was simply a victim. What impact might that experience have on how she feels as a person, on her confidence and her ability to assert herself?

Far to the south, toward the end of a recent school year in Birmingham, Alabama, a third-grade boy came home one afternoon with a stamp on his arm. It was the image of a smiley face, with words written below. The boy's father, Jon Bivens, at first thought it was a "good job" stamp, but then was stunned when he read the words: "I need lunch money." An angry Bivens called it "branding" and kept his son home for the last few days of the year.

Strangely, this shaming came when the Bivens account was still in the black, though with a balance of only $1.38. From the school's perspective, it was akin to sending a notice that a library book would soon be overdue. The stamps sent home on children's arms were an innovative way to remind parents to replenish their accounts. This was based on impeccable logic. The balance was approaching zero. Communication was needed. Stamps transmitted the message.

Shame? That didn't enter into the calculation, at least not explicitly. But shame exerts invisible power over people, and many parents would cough up the money rather than draw attention to their poverty.

Like weight shame and addiction shame, poverty shame creates toxic feedback loops. A person who is ashamed of her poverty is likely to respond in one of two ways: by hiding the problem or acting as though it doesn't exist. Both approaches are fueled by shame, and both tend to make it worse.

Hiding is known as "withdrawal." It's easy enough to understand. Imagine calling a friend you haven't seen in a while to go to a movie or grab a bite somewhere. You're unaware that he has no money, a pile of unpaid bills, and massive debt. Is he going to tell you that? Most people don't. As Neal Gabler wrote in *The Atlantic*, men are more likely to discuss their experiences with Viagra than their credit card debt. In other words, poverty may be even more shameful than sexual impotence. So there's an excellent chance that the friend you're calling will come up with some reason other than personal finances to say no to the outing.

Withdrawal leads to isolation. It burns bridges between people who might otherwise make common cause. One friend might know about a job opportunity or someone who can help with childcare. Another might have a cousin at a county food kitchen. Isolation destroys this web of social capital. Research by Arnoud Plantinga, a Dutch social psychologist, traces the resulting spiral downward. Withdrawal deepens as it leads to more poverty and shame. On and on it goes. Worse yet, loneliness often leads to depression, which in turn feeds the expanding sense of hopelessness.

The opposite tendency, by no means healthier, is "approach." This occurs, according to Plantinga, when a person attempts to cast off the shame of poverty by reclaiming lost status. If that struggling friend you call chooses to approach rather than withdraw, he may insist on going to a fancy restaurant, where he would order a $150 bottle of Russian vodka, throw down his credit card, and leave the waiter a 30 percent tip. Steeped in denial, this behavior salves the emotional wounds of poverty but only for the moment. It's unsustainable, of course, and the victim digs further into the pit of poverty and shame.

This raises the common refrain that the poor are responsible for their condition, because, from the perspective of the more comfortable classes, they tend to make bad decisions. Yet desperate situations have their own logic. People suffering from poverty face pain on two fronts: physical and psychic. Many not only lack basic human needs—food, clothing, shelter, and transportation—but are made to feel terrible about it. Shame is a threat to their very existence. When each day poses urgent challenges, strategies for next month or next year remain largely theoretical. So yes, it might make sense to forgo a $10 rotisserie chicken and instead boil a $1 head of cabbage—assuming there's a nearby grocery store with fresh produce—and put $9 into savings. But to make that calculation, a person must have faith in a future furnished with upward stairways and exit doors. For many, that is akin to believing in fairies. So as Plantinga's research demonstrates, many poor people's thinking tends to focus on trade-offs in the here and now. This undermines the scant chance they have to advance and earns them yet more shame.

It's enough to make you wonder what a smart and caring society could possibly do. The lasting solution, which is almost impossible to imagine in the United States, is to provide everyone with a solid education, housing, and childcare so that everyone can pursue jobs on an equal footing. After all, a job with decent pay and benefits not only promises to lift people out of poverty but also can confer a sense of pride. This isn't to say that people need a career to have a sense of self-worth. But steady employment offers an antidote to poverty shame.

This was the idea behind the landmark welfare reform that President Bill Clinton signed into law shortly before his reelection in 1996. The goal was to lead people, with a combination of sticks and carrots, from public assistance to employment and self-sufficiency. At the signing ceremony, Clinton said that the new law "should represent not simply the ending of a system that too often hurts those it is supposed to help, but the beginning of a new era in which welfare will become what it was meant to be: a second chance, not a way of life."

The bill, however, did not spell out the groundwork necessary for such a transformation and left the details largely up to the states. Most of them provided little or nothing in the way of funding for job training or childcare and simply mandated job hunts, often to a ludicrous degree. Georgia, for example, kicked people off assistance if they failed to document sixty job applications per week or attend eight job preparation sessions.

Despite these problems, the effect was not entirely negative. Millions actually found jobs. And many of these people still benefit from government funding, the so-called Earned Income Tax Credit. This policy hoists many working families with children above the poverty line. But it also props up employers like Walmart and fast-food restaurants, enabling them to keep paying starvation wages. More than that, it provides statistical grounding for defenders of the shame-based status quo. It backs their contention that the poor can work their way out of abject poverty—and that those who fall short are responsible for their plight.

Sadly, welfare reform has created a nucleus of poor people who are now much worse off than before. Failing to satisfy the job requirement or other paperwork, they have fallen off the shrinking welfare rolls and plunged deeper into poverty, leading many to homelessness, prison, and addiction. When Clinton's reforms were introduced in 1996, sixty-eight out of one hundred families living below the poverty line received assistance. Now only twenty-three do. And that segment has grown poorer. A University of Michigan study, for example, found that the number of American households living in the deepest poverty—defined by a rock-bottom income of less than $2 per day per inhabitant—more than doubled in the fifteen years after welfare reform passed, from 636,000 to 1.46 million. Children are disproportionately represented in the category. Only the most exceptionally resilient among them grow up believing that they have a chance, and even fewer manage to claw their way up. Again, the rare success stories are held up as evidence that those left behind are to blame for their failures.

But what happens when being left behind becomes the norm? The economic battle spurred by the COVID-19 pandemic brought fresh thinking to poverty, stripping away some of the shame. During the first economic shutdown, in 2020, millions of workers lost their jobs. With that, the "unemployed" shed the stigma of "lazy," at least for a time. So the jobless received checks, without having to demonstrate how needy they were or how hard they were trying to find work. This was progress. A year later, a host of features in the jumbo stimulus package President Biden signed into law provided unconditional aid, especially to families with children. This promised to lift many kids out of poverty. But that didn't stop the conservative American Enterprise Institute from warning that the new assistance could lead "more than one third of unmarried women [to] reduce their employment by at least one hour per week." This recapitulates the Reagan-era thinking that gave us welfare queens: If we stop punching down on the poor for being poor, they'll get lazy.*

———————

Our society, it seems, is engineered so that even institutions designed to help the poor end up punching down on them, sometimes mercilessly. Take the case of the New York–based nonprofit Center for Employment Opportunities, Inc., or CEO. Founded in 1970, the company focuses on helping ex-convicts make the transition to the outside world and, crucially, gain skills so they can find jobs. As the company itself describes it:

> CEO's mission is grounded [on the assumption] that if formerly incarcerated individuals are provided structured employment interventions when they are immediately released from prison or jail, they are more likely to break the cycle of recidivism and to build a positive foundation for themselves and their families. CEO exists to create greater opportunity for people who are systematically excluded from realizing economic success.

What's not to like? This laudable mission helped CEO garner $21 million in charitable contributions in 2017, according to its most recent financial report. That accounted for 40 percent of its revenue.

And yet, when you talk to former inmates who looked to CEO for job opportunities and guidance, they describe a hellish experience,

———

*This perspective became all too clear during the COVID-19 pandemic, when a host of Republican governors blamed worker shortages in low-wage industries on unemployment checks and pulled the plug on the federally funded emergency aid.

featuring threats, coercion, poverty, and degradation—in short, life inside a shame machine. Take the experience of Duane Townes. In 2013, he was freed on parole after serving most of his seven-year term for attempted burglary in Eastern Correctional Facility, a state prison one hundred miles north of New York City. He was fifty-two years old. It wasn't Townes's first stint in prison. But this time, he says, he was determined to make the most of his next chance on the outside. The key to success, he knew, was to land a decent job that paid a living wage. With this in mind, he had undergone job training in prison and had earned certification in asbestos removal. This was one of the nastiest jobs in construction, but the surest path, as he saw it, to a union job with benefits.

Townes's parole officer directed him to CEO in New York City. The prospect was supremely unappealing. But Townes felt that to ignore this decree and pursue another path might have landed him back in prison for violation of parole. So he went. Upon reporting there, Townes learned, to his disappointment, that his training and certification counted for nothing, at least at CEO. He had to establish himself with much cruder tasks. "They slotted me to a job where I'm walking along a highway, on Staten Island, just picking up debris," he says. His take-home pay for a full day of this work was $48.

Other jobs included cleaning bathrooms at government facilities, mopping, and other janitorial tasks. He compared this existence to prison: It was "basically a work camp, where you don't feel you exist."

The difference, though, was that Townes had a roof over his head and three meals a day in prison, while his meager income at CEO failed to cover even basic expenses. He had to spend Fridays with his job coach, unpaid, where he would "talk about his experience." That left his weekly pay at less than $200. While he was able to bunk for free at his mother's apartment, the money was barely enough for MetroCards and food. "It was a blow to my ego," he says.

During this ordeal, whether on work crews or with their job coach, Townes and his fellow workers were under steady surveillance. If anyone showed signs of rebelling, the coach or foreman could report them to their parole officers. "You're not thinking about the money," says David Robinson, another alumnus of the same program. "You're thinking about doing what parole says, and not getting into trouble and getting sent back. [CEO uses] it to their advantage. 'You do this or we're going to call your parole officer.' It's a nightmare."

"I wasn't treated like a man," says Duane Townes. But like the others in his crew, he was in a precarious position. To stay out on parole, he needed to maintain a job. He didn't have the luxury of being able to quit working at CEO in order to hunt for something better. "You stay there until CEO deems that you're ready to leave," he says.

And who would make that decision? For Townes, it was his job coach, a former convict who had worked his way up through the CEO system, from mopping and garbage duty to manager, a salaried position. "For him, it's a power game," Townes says. "There's a dominant person and a servile one. It's like master and slave."

In 2012, an influential social policy think tank, MDRC, wrote a glowing report on CEO that helped fuel its explosive growth, and the organization expanded across the country. (CEO now operates in thirty cities across eleven states and opened offices as recently as 2020 in Fresno, California, and Charlotte, North Carolina.) In the paper, MDRC argued that by sending paroled felons on closely supervised work crews, CEO helped them develop "soft skills," such as showing up on time and following orders.

Those who fare best in the CEO system, according to quotes in the MDRC report, are parolees who stoop to their lowly lot and accept enforced poverty. The apparent goal is to drill home the message that they don't deserve anything better. Consider these quotes attributed to the program's successes:

> "It's better than six cents an hour. You can't just come out of prison and then expect for somebody to [say], 'Here, we have this $70,000-a-year job for you because you just got out of prison.' It doesn't work like that."
> "When my parole officer told me about the daily paycheck [at CEO], even though it's $40 a day, it helps."
> "You get paid every day. I mean, it's not a lot of money, but it's some money."
> "I just learned self-control, patience, and how to respect the higher authority, you know?"

What if one of these workers had pushed for more money or moved to organize fellow parolees? According to Tamir Rosenblum, a union lawyer in New York who works with previously incarcerated folks, "it seems certain he would have been deemed to have engaged in 'distorted thinking,' violated 'core correctional practices,' and posed an elevated risk of giving in to his criminal urges."

CEO's approach, after all, is based upon the assumption that menial work under close supervision delivers therapeutic value. A 2016 MDRC report spells this out. Parolees leave prison, according to the report, with "criminogenic needs." These include risk factors such as impulsivity, lack of self-control, aggression, and antisocial peers. CEO contends that they suffer from "cognitive distortions," which are learned but can be changed. And CEO's system accomplishes that by applying "techniques similar to those commonly used in cognitive behavioral therapy."

It may be the case that a number of parolees emerge from prison with bad work habits. Some of them have drug issues. Many lack skills and education. The question, though, is whether it's a sound strategy—let alone a compassionate one—to place them in a work environment that feels, at least to some of them, like slavery, and at rock-bottom pay. "If I'd have stayed there, I would have ended up back in prison," says Townes. "Finances would have pushed me to crime."

Much like other shame machines, this one justifies its practices with highly questionable statistics. The 2016 report, for example, trumpets CEO's "impressive" results in reducing recidivism, but provides no data to back up this claim. The earlier 2012 study acknowledges that CEO did not improve employment or earn-ings thirty-six months following program entry. But it makes the claim that the program significantly reduced recidivism, especially "among those most recently released from prison." In other words, while the parolees are picking up garbage and mopping floors under the watchful eyes of their chiefs, they're less likely to com-mit crimes.

There's scant evidence that recidivism is reduced by the CEO program in the long term. And no wonder: It's part of the larger post-prison employment system's dysfunctionality. A study by UCLA law professor Noah Zatz chronicles the "double bind" that formerly incarcerated folks have to contend with: discrimination based on their record and pressure to accept work based on the threat from their parole officers. As a result, they are systematically underpaid and must put up with bad or terrible conditions at work. Many of them naturally revert to their former livelihoods, which eventually land them back in jail.

This noxious feedback loop recalls a similar one on *The Big-gest Loser*. As we saw, obese people shed hundreds of pounds while under the supervision of trainers who led them on starva-tion diets and through frenetic exercise regimens. But that weight loss—much like a forced-labor program that pays $192 a week—is unsustainable. Like CEO, it breeds recidivism. Parolees who fail to adapt to CEO's transition program that virtually enslaves them are trundled back to prison. That way, CEO keeps its pipeline full.

This punishing approach, using the penal system to repress workers, has poisoned labor relations, especially in the South, for more than a century. Douglas A. Blackmon's 2009 Pulitzer Prize–winning history *Slavery by Another Name* details how in the nineteenth century legislators passed so-called Black Codes, which mandated that all freedmen be employed. Those who weren't could be charged with vagrancy and condemned to work on plantations, in forestry, or in mines.

We might expect this from right-wing politicians who campaign against welfare cheats and blame the poor for their lot. What's noteworthy about CEO, however, is that it is sustained by pillars of the northern liberal establishment. Sam Schaeffer, who earns nearly $300,000 per year as executive director of CEO, formerly served as director of economic development for New York's senior Democratic senator, Charles Schumer, the chamber's majority leader. MDRC's funders include a wide range of philanthropies, from the public arm of JPMorgan Chase to the Bill & Melinda Gates Foundation. These people believe they're helping.

And this raises a key point. Most of us, even with the best intentions, accept the premises and promises of the shame machines operating all around us. We find it hard to believe, for example, that executives at Weight Watchers aren't dedicated to addressing obesity, or that the punishing regime at CEO, while tough, isn't what those convicts need. Sure, if we take the time to study statistics, we might see that they're problematic. But the people in charge mean well, don't they?

Many of them do. But they're operating within ecosystems ruled by shame—and propped up by pseudoscientific research.

One such study, which masterfully shifts blame onto the poor in the name of objectivity, is known as the marshmallow experiment. Administered by Walter Mischel, a psychologist at Stanford in the 1960s, it attempted to gauge young children's capacity to master self-control.

Mischel and his colleagues launched the experiment at a Stanford nursery school. Each child was given a marshmallow and told that they could eat it immediately. However, if they managed to resist the temptation and leave it intact, they would be awarded a second marshmallow later. A third of the children turned a deaf ear to these promises and ate the treat immediately. Another third tried to wait but didn't make it to fifteen minutes. And the final group, young masters of delayed gratification, were waiting with marshmallows untouched when the researchers returned.

For Mischel, the marshmallow study was about the ability to understand time and to plan. Some children appeared to be better at it than others. He had two daughters in the school, and he asked them, as the years passed, how their classmates were faring. The results seemed to confirm his hypothesis. The students who had waited for the second marshmallow appeared to be thriving, getting better grades and higher scores on standardized tests. Later studies indicated that they went on to lead more successful lives. Statistically, those who had demonstrated an ability to postpone gratification progressed further in school and stayed in better physical shape. They saved money. Fewer of their marriages ended in divorce. Discipline, it appeared, was a harbinger of success. And wouldn't you know? White kids from prosperous families fared better than poor minority children.

What was wrong with those kids who had wolfed down the first marshmallow? Had they been raised with the wrong values? Was it genetics? In either case, thinking ahead was a crucial skill, and they appeared to be missing it.

People have been blaming the poor for their lot for millennia, often attributing their woes to poor self-control and bad decisions: "The wise store up choice food and olive oil," says the Bible. "But fools gulp theirs down." This was an attractive conclusion for the ruling classes. The marshmallow study appeared to confirm what they already believed: that they raised kids with the right stuff, both genetic and cultural, while the underclasses came up disastrously short. Everyone therefore was where they belonged, and the rich were not to blame. What's more, spending additional money to help the poor certainly wouldn't help. They'd no doubt squander it just as impetuously as their kids gobbled marshmallows.

This self-serving analysis, bolstered by questionable science, sustained the status quo and shamed the poor. But conclusions drawn from the marshmallow study crumbled under further scrutiny. In 2018, scientists replicated the experiment on a scale ten times as large, while controlling for the parents' income and education. What they found was that the wealth and education of a child's parents correlated far more closely to long-term success than anything to do with eating a marshmallow.

It was true that the poorer children were less likely to postpone gratification. But there were good reasons for this. Children raised in prosperity tend to take material promises from scientists in white coats as gospel, because their parents have always had the wherewithal to deliver. Poor kids, by contrast, have reason for doubt. Life has taught them about scarcity. There may be nothing in the refrigerator for breakfast tomorrow. For them, perhaps, a sure thing at this moment trumps a promised payoff down the road. In some scenarios, this is both prudent and smart. It's the certainty of a bird in the hand over the possibility of two in the bush. Similarly, if they've seen their parents mistrust authority, whether it's the social workers who deny their needs or the doctors who ignore their pain, then it stands to reason the children, too, will greet the promises of this stranger offering marshmallows with skepticism.

As obvious as these cultural considerations might appear, a nuanced perspective has little power to overturn the dominant punching-down narrative. So the wealthy majority continues to stipulate that only people who work deserve help. And miserly benefits continue to subsidize the disgracefully low wages paid by fast-food restaurants and retail giants. In this way, society keeps the working poor on a hamster wheel, struggling mightily just to get by, with no money to spare if their car breaks down or their kid gets sick. And it condemns the unemployed poor to abject poverty. In short, it punishes people for failure and accepts their misery as the status quo.

This is both shortsighted and immoral. The key to changing it—which goes against all of our shaming instincts—is to help people in need, and to stop making assistance contingent on work. Poor people, like everyone else, should have childcare, shelter, healthcare, food, and access to decent education. They should not have to grovel before one bureaucracy or another, or satisfy a list of prerequisites, for these essentials.

What's more, work requirements all too often compound the problem. Imagine a young man recently released from prison. It's in society's interest, as well as his own, for him to pursue training as a mechanic at a local trade school, to help take care of his four-year-old son, and, perhaps, to take his grandmother to her sessions at the dialysis center. Yet if those activities preclude him from a long commute to a minimum-wage job at a big-box store, he risks losing the skimpy benefits he might have qualified for. As society punches down on him, he and his family suffer. To roll back poverty shame, we simply must help the poor, without questions or conditions.

CHAPTER 4

"YOUR VAGINA IS FINE"

American women had reason to worry. As all the magazines told them, this was an issue so intimate and drenched in shame that even mentioning it was almost impossible. But if they didn't deal with it right away, they could lose their marriage! "I guess I was really to blame when Stan started paying attention to other women," a fictional wife confessed in a 1954 advertisement unearthed by BuzzFeed's Krista Torres. "It wasn't that I didn't know about feminine hygiene. I had become . . . well . . . *forgetful*."

This character's growing fear, though she would never use such words, was that her husband was disgusted by the smell of her vagina. The way to rekindle their romance was to scrub her vulva with a chemical so toxic that it would exterminate any biological activity capable of producing odor. With nothing less than her marriage at stake, she would make use of the same poisonous disinfectant that she used on the toilet: Lysol.

With that dramatic step, she won back her husband.

These shaming tactics found their market. Many women in the first half of the twentieth century douched with Lysol. The original manufacturer—a New York company called Lehn & Fink—assured them that disinfecting their crotch would not only ease their husbands' revulsion to natural processes of the female body but also be perfectly safe.

This, of course, was a lie. Until the 1950s, Lysol contained cresol, a potent methylphenol that damages human flesh and is especially punishing to sensitive mucous membranes—eyes, mouth, genitalia. Yet to save their marriage, women were urged to attack their vulvas like a dirty sink. "It reaches deeply into folds and crevices to search out germs," the advertisement boasted. (That much was true. Many women, in fact, used Lysol in the vain hope that the germ killer would work as a contraceptive.)

Lysol's marketing strategy shamed half of humanity for the by-products of a functioning reproductive system. Women suffered from painful burns and blisters. Some died. But suing the manufacturer, and discussing these intimate matters on public record, was not going to happen.

This is why our sexual organs are prime targets for shame machines. They generate profound fears and insecurities within us. Even in these more sexually liberated times we tend to envelop them in secrecy.

Private shame makes people vulnerable to campaigns built on suggestion and innuendo. Those old Lysol ads merely raised the possibility that something might be terribly amiss, that others might be whispering about it, maybe cracking jokes. In the magazine advertisement, Stan clearly hadn't told his wife that she grossed him out. He just started drifting away. How many other women were in the same bind? How many swabbed with Lysol and hurt themselves to address a problem they were only imagining?

That might seem like ancient history, but the shame market that Lysol focused on—the embarrassing imperfections of our own bodies—is richer than ever. Americans spend $40 billion a year on health supplements, from pills to powders, to pack on muscle, look fresh, or retain their masculinity or femininity (whichever is being sold). The supply now features fifty thousand products, a tenfold increase over the past two decades.

Supplements represent only one segment of the sprawling

wellness industry. It's a complex that addresses, with everything from scented gels to self-help podcasts, any aspect of our lives where our performance is less than optimal. These fixes can be physical, cosmetic, emotional, financial, or spiritual. But all of them spring from the simple premise that most of us are subpar: ugly, sick, smelly, sexually inadequate, too old, too foolish with money. There has to be something we hate about ourselves, and these companies make sure we find it. The commercial possibilities are limitless. And like the other shame domains we've explored, the wellness sector brims with phony science, bad statistics, and false promises.

Some players in this vast industry simply update toxic messaging from the past. Consider Vagisil. As its name suggests, the company focuses on the same hygiene market that Lysol targeted nearly a century ago. Founded by women, Vagisil promotes itself as a straight-shooting, taboo-busting advocate for women's bodies. The company's mission statement explicitly confronts the shame of earlier decades: "Empowering women to be more open about vaginal health and seek the solutions they need since 1973. Without apology. Without stigma. Without shame." Yet a lucrative and growing branch of Vagisil's business follows the old Lysol template, suggesting to women that they smell awful and badly need a chemical scrub. This line of feminine hygiene, writes Jen Gunter, an OB/GYN and author of *The Vagina Bible*, "taps into a primal fear about reproductive tract cleanliness, and it's a gold mine."

One especially promising market for this fear campaign is the adolescent. She is new to her adult body and often brimming with insecurities. If anyone can be easily convinced that she might need some perfuming down there, it's a teenager. In the summer of 2020, Vagisil launched a new product line for teens, OMV!, and bolstered it with an energetic social media campaign. The overt message was that girls should be proud of their bodies, including their vaginas. True enough. But that was simply the opening to alert girls to potential problems brewing. Were these very young women by any chance aware of "period funk," a certain odor that followed menstruation? Someone might be emitting this stink and not know it. We humans, after all, are notoriously insensitive to our own smell, and even our close friends are often too embarrassed to bring it up with us. So if there's even a trace of odor in your panties, girls are told, other people might be picking up on it in a big way and ridiculing you.

Keep your chin up, is Vagisil's friendly advice: "Vaginal odor happens to all of us, but it shouldn't stop you from doing you. So the next time you're wondering if you're the only fragrant woman in Pilates, know that you're not and that there's no shame in your game." The company claims to have worked with teens to come up with all kinds of wipes and gels that are "gentle, convenient, and smell really good." Vagisil's young customers can imbue their vulvas with the fragrance of peach blossom, white jasmine, and cucumber magnolia. With a dry wash spray called Odor Block, they can even attack odor before it gets started.

On its Instagram feed, the campaign artfully blends a defiant anti-stigma message with the implication that girls have good reason to worry every single month. "Periods are beautiful, powerful, and should never be stigmatized. . . . PERIODT.* Enter for a chance to snag an OMV! goodie bag for you and a friend, so you can both feel fresh and confident all month . . ."

The OMV! campaign infuriates many in the medical community, who spot the shame machine and see through its phony science. Gunter argues that women risk damaging themselves by applying chemicals to the vulva, and that the safest approach is

---

*PERIODT is slang spelling that puts emphasis on a point.

to stick with water. Jocelyn J. Fitzgerald, a surgeon and professor at the University of Pittsburgh Medical Center's Magee-Womens Hospital, notes that the OMV! campaign creates a brilliant self-sustaining shame market. "Using their products while your vagina is perfectly fine will destroy your microbiome, give you real Bacterial Vaginosis, and prompt you to buy more Vagisil," she tweets. "Don't fall for it girls," she adds. "Your vagina is fine."

For most of human history, beauty was not something people achieved but instead a gift of the gods. Consider the Greek myth of Helen of Troy. She was reputed in antiquity to be the loveliest woman in the world. When Paris, a Trojan prince, abducted her from Sparta and spirited her away to Troy, all of Greece went to war to win her back. Her mother was a princess named Leda, whose beauty was unrivaled. Her father, Zeus, was so smitten by Leda's beauty that he turned himself into a swan and raped her. This was (perverse) punishment for simply existing as a woman. Helen, the offspring of such exotic lineage, didn't have to suffer Botox injections or clear her pores with a charcoal mask. Her beauty was preordained.

Today's shame machines have turned destiny on its head. Thanks to science, technology, and cutting-edge surgical techniques, we in theory can vanquish our natural defects and achieve beauty and balance. With anti-aging creams, body sculpting, scientifically tailored diets rich in antioxidants, therapies to find our child within or to optimize sleep, we have gained the power to ward away ugliness and even the ravages of time. If we use these interventions correctly, we can approach the perfection of the gods.

The flip side of this message is obvious: If we fail to address our shortcomings in any way, that's on us. Much like the other shame machines we've explored, from poverty to addiction, this one boils down to choices. The right ones, by design, cost a lot of money. But if we make dumb choices and carry on with our defects, it's our fault.

Today, there is no single exemplar of the ideal, a modern Helen of Troy. Our market is too vast and varied. But for a sprawling demographic of reality TV fans, Kim Kardashian fits the bill. Her body is like a fantasy cartoon for sexual appeal. Her large breasts appear as perfect spheres. Her torso curves down to a tiny waist and then balloons into broad hips and a disproportionate ass that would struggle as much as mine with an economy-class seat on a plane—not that Kim Kardashian would ever have to fly economy.

Kim Kardashian's body is central to both her brand and her commercial empire. Her very profitable company is currently called KKW Beauty, and it sells makeup, lipstick, and other cosmetics. By early 2020 Kardashian's fortune was creeping toward billionaire status and in April 2021 it was achieved. The founding assumption of her business is that looks are not God-given. It's a never-ending job. And it's expensive. One branch of her branded enterprise involves pitching shelves of products designed to help lesser mortals achieve the perfection of the Kardashian body. For a single Instagram post, she rakes in an estimated half million dollars. She pops up on millions of feeds, promoting Flat Tummy appetite-suppressing lollipops; Fit Tea, a fourteen-day detox program; SugarBearHair gummy vitamins to improve locks' luster and richness; and many more aspirational offerings.

She sells fantasy. And the marketing is based on shame: having anything less than a dream body is a choice. If you don't like what you were born with, you can fix it. It's up to you. This is a powerful message, especially for young women. Their anxiety regarding these issues is unrelenting, and it begins early. Fifty-three percent of thirteen-year-old American girls are unhappy with their bodies, according to a study by the Park Nicollet Melrose Center in

Minnesota, and this number explodes to 78 percent by the time they reach seventeen.

These fears fuel endless business for sex goddesses like Kim Kardashian. To inch closer to their ideal, millions of women strive, worry, work out, diet, buy all kinds of branded garbage, and yet never achieve their goal of looking like her. Many of them feel like wrecks. Beauty has long been the perfect scam, an inexhaustible shame machine.

It's an age-old conflict for women. If they don't buy sufficiently into the beauty standard, they hazard being ostracized as ugly. But even if they manage to reach Kardashian levels of glamour, they will still face sexual expectations and stigma.

Shaming women for their sexuality has been a tool of patri-archies across cultures and centuries. This is most pronounced in rape trials, where the defense attorney asks the victim what she was wearing, suggesting that she encouraged the crime and is a slut. The woman cannot control the narrative. If she is expected to be beautiful, but runs the risk of overdoing it and thus inviting rape (precisely Leda's crisis vis-à-vis Zeus), how much power does she have over her own body and existence? Some things haven't changed since the Trojan War. Body approval, especially for young women, is painfully contingent on, and bound tightly to, the urges and whims of a society run by men.

The woman on the receiving end of this drumbeat of advice, it goes without saying, needs help, probably badly. She is not being kind to her body. She can't help but see herself as impure, someone who has fallen out of step with nature, and is paying the price, whether the trouble surfaces as diminished libido, wrinkles, insom-nia, anxiety, bad breath, or cankles.

Wellness, like other shame machines we've seen, voices nothing but the best intentions. At the forefront of the industry is Goop, founded in 2008 by the actress Gwyneth Paltrow as a "homespun weekly newsletter." According to Goop, "We operate from a place of curiosity and nonjudgment, and we start hard conversations, crack open taboos, and look for connection and resonance everywhere we can find it." The company, with an estimated value of $250 million in 2019, sells expensive elixirs to aid sleep and tighten wrinkled skin. Goop even offers spiritual check-ins for "releasing old energy, realigning with your purpose, or just taking a beat to be instead of do."

As with weight-loss and addiction treatments, many of Goop's claims are anchored in bullshit science. In 2018, for example, California regulators won a settlement from Goop after suing for false advertising. The company had sold a $66 vaginal jade egg with the promise that by inserting it, like a tampon, women could regulate menstrual cycles, balance hormones, and improve bladder control.

The implicit message in this marketing was that intelligent women who took care of their bodies would buy this egg and reap its benefits. And all the others, suffering from hormonal jags or getting up three or four times in the night to pee? They didn't know what was good for them.

Perhaps the most perverse segment of the wellness industry is the enormous arsenal of products and services designed to camouflage aging, or better, to postpone or reverse it. The premise undergirding the entire industry is that aging is a disaster. Old people are weak, ugly, wrinkled, out of touch, pathetic, moribund. To be old in our society is to be shamed.

If you're not convinced, then why do people over thirty or so lie about their age in only one direction? "You look young" is a compliment. "I feel old" is likewise a sign of defeat. To tell a person directly that he or she looks old would be beyond rude, and that's why we don't see it happen very often, but make no mistake: ageism is pervasive even if not overt.

Most other shame machines subsist on the contempt we have for others. We participate, often unwittingly, by punching down on those who have screwed up, as we see it, making wrong or lazy choices. They eat too much. They don't work. They take drugs. They waste money. We direct shame, as a matter of course, toward people behaving badly.

But ageism is different. Old age is where all of us are heading. Like it or not, those of us who don't want to die young intend to grow old. So shaming the old is a warped form of self-loathing. We hate and disrespect what we're going to become—and work fiercely to push it back.

Ashton Applewhite, an anti-ageism activist and author, argues that ageism is a venomous obsession. To stave it off, we feed shame machines. In Silicon Valley, she says, "engineers are getting Botox and hair plugs before key interviews. And these are skilled white men in their thirties, so imagine the effects further down the food chain."

Perhaps the scariest affliction associated with aging is dementia. Losing dominion of the mind and memory is a visceral fear. Adding to it is the sense that other people are witnessing their decline, picking up on every pause, every misplaced word. So much of the shame is internal and projected. That doesn't dull its power or its market potential. If people find a product that promises to keep the mind intact and the memory sound, Applewhite says, it's a buy.

Mark Underwood grasped this early on. While still in his twenties, the former psychology major at the University of Wisconsin–Milwaukee devised a miracle drug based on a jellyfish protein called apoaequorin. It is similar in structure to calcium-binding proteins that regulate calcium in the human brain. The idea was to create a pill that would be swallowed and digested, with a synthetic version of the jellyfish protein then traveling up to the head. If it could reduce the buildup of calcium in arteries outside the brain, it might slow or even reverse the effects of dementia. The effectiveness of apoaequorin was (and would remain) more of an inkling than proven science. But loads of people, Underwood hoped, would pay to delay the onset of forgetfulness. He would brand his pills as Prevagen.

In his 1991 Wisconsin high school yearbook, Underwood had vowed to "make a totally obnoxious amount of money at an early age and spend the rest of my life spending it," according to a *Wired* magazine investigative article. In 2004, Underwood, then thirty years old, teamed up with a local businessman in Milwaukee, Michael Beaman, to launch Quincy Bioscience. The following year they founded Prevagen. Much of the initial marketing was by phone. Picture a call center full of people contacting long lists of older folks and asking them whether a name or a fact ever seemed to play hide-and-seek. Their pitch would repeat the spiel about jellyfish and the putative powers of their proteins. They would cite cognitive studies (sponsored by the company) and offer a month's supply for $50 or $60. The business took off.

Quincy Bioscience was careful to register Prevagen as a supplement, not a pharmaceutical. This eased the regulatory oversight. Supplements have to clear a lower hurdle, establishing only that they don't cause damage—hurting or killing the consumer. Whether they actually work is not an issue.

But false claims still mattered. And as Prevagen expanded its market, regulators and consumer advocates began to focus critical attention on extravagant claims Quincy was making on its website and Facebook page. The company stated that Prevagen was the "first and only dietary supplement that . . . protects the brain cells from death." At the same time, Quincy leaned into the shame angle, promising that Prevagen "will restore for you the lost protein so that you can gain your dignity back."

The Food and Drug Administration issued a warning to Quincy

Bioscience in 2012, and the Federal Trade Commission sued the same year for false advertising. Plaintiff's attorneys have jumped in with class actions. In the meantime, thousands of customers have filed complaints of side effects, ranging from arrhythmia to hallucinations. All of this has kept Quincy's lawyers extremely busy. And yet, the company has managed to build Prevagen into a mainstream product. The pills are now available at Walgreens, at CVS, and on Amazon. The company has also inserted its magic protein into foods, launching NeuroShake in 2013—instead of keeping you up, like a cup of coffee or a Red Bull, it enhances brain health: "Kick start your mind!"

Quincy Bioscience now spends heavily on TV advertising. Friendly older people stand in for the jilted wife in the old Lysol ads. They have a confession to make. Before Prevagen, they found themselves struggling to remember names and other facts. They were losing it, and it was embarrassing. They couldn't bring themselves to share the truth, not even with their best friends. But then they found a product, a pill called Prevagen, and, what do you know, the old memory is feeling fresh!

There's scant evidence that the drug actually does what it promises to do. As Robert Shmerling, a professor at Harvard Medical School, writes, "And if apoaequorin is so great, why aren't jellyfish smarter, as a colleague of mine wonders?" Quincy Bioscience, like other shame machines, responds to such questions with phony science. According to Mark Underwood, in 2010 the company carried out "[a] large double blind, placebo-controlled trial that . . . showed great efficacy for Prevagen, showing statistically significant improvements in word recall, in executive function, and also in short term memory." The so-called Madison Memory Study involved 218 subjects, who were given either ten milligrams of Prevagen or a placebo. The subjects were then assessed on nine cognitive tasks over ninety days. According to the FTC's complaint against Prevagen, the results represented a setback for the company. They showed no statistically significant improvement.

But phony science can recast a bad result to make it a good one. Nothing to worry about. The trick is for statisticians to dive into the data, slicing and dicing until they can cobble together something better. In their hunt for "significant" results, the company conducted more than thirty different analyses of the Madison Memory Study findings, breaking down each of the nine cognitive tasks into smaller subgroups. This is a classic technique for lying with statistics, and the people who did this study either knew they were lying or shouldn't have been employed as statisticians. By breaking large data sets into increments, manipulators benefit from the nature of small numbers. If you were to flip a penny a hundred times, the results would usually come close to 50-50. And if you flipped a thousand times, that balance would be even more likely. But if you divide that series of one hundred into ten subgroups, many of them will show deviations. A couple of the samples are likely to show 8 to 2, or at least 7 to 3. Those who fudge statistics zero in on the samples that fit their conclusions.

———

The dynamics of our shame dramas, up to this point, have been as clear-cut as a medieval morality play. These immense shame machines punch down on people to exploit their obesity, addiction, poverty, or suboptimal health, gaining power and market share in the process. They treat their victims as lucrative business targets or as utterly disposable—and often combine both tactics. The rest of us maintain this status quo by accepting as gospel its false premises: The losers deserve their fate because they've made bad choices; maybe if they feel bad enough they'll fix it. Shame is powerful, and it works—even when it shouldn't.

We must come to grips with these powerful shame industries, because they perpetuate dysfunctional status quos, and profit from them, while solving nothing. Obesity rates are skyrocketing. Opioids are ravaging urban and rural communities. Obscene numbers of young Black men are languishing in prison. Inequality has reached heights not seen since the Gilded Age. Shame is at work in each of these societal failures, and yet it also functions as a distraction mechanism. When faced with the problems, we're offered an easy out again and again: If only those people didn't make such disastrous choices, they wouldn't be suffering. It's *their* fault. So the shame spiral rolls on, and things get worse.

How do we disrupt these ruinous cycles? The first step is to build awareness. We need a reckoning. Most of us accept the status quo and hardly perceive the punching down that sustains it. We can unveil the underlying nastiness by looking at the world around us, our relationships and the dynamics of power, through the lens of shame.

We've taken steps in this direction before, with racism and sexism. I'm not holding up our track record on either as a smashing success. But there is growing awareness of both, which is necessary for reform. As recently as the 1960s, barely a half century ago, there were virtually no Black people on network TV shows or the news, much less in advertisements. And that, apparently, did not bother white audiences, because no one had forced them to recognize how bizarrely unrepresentative it was. During the same decade, only a small contingent of feminists would have stopped to consider how unjust it was that of the twenty-eight cabinet members who served under President Lyndon Johnson, there was not a single woman.

A similar blindness afflicts us when it comes to confronting the giant shame machines that we nurture. However, if millions of us start to break apart the machines to see their inner workings, attitudes can change—in the public, in the media, in corporations, and in politics. Then we can take steps toward righting the wrongs.

The psychologist Donna Hicks offers a useful framework for

thinking this through. For many years, Hicks has worked on conflict resolution in countries around the world. She has sat with warring parties in the Middle East, in Sri Lanka, in Colombia, trying to help them establish common ground and work toward peace.

What she found below all of the arguments were deep undercurrents of pain. Often both sides in a negotiation felt demeaned, brushed off, excluded, disrespected by those across the table. Hicks determined that people could never forge agreements without honoring one another's dignity as human beings.

She went on to study and enumerate what she called dignity violations. Her idea is that all of us, upon birth, are open, vulnerable, and, of course, worthy of respect from others. But as we experience contempt, exclusion, and distrust—when we are, in effect, shamed—we harden, protecting ourselves. Shame, and not dignity, becomes the emotional currency of our realm. As a society, we participate, often unwittingly, and perpetuate the punishment by punching down. And the pitiless shame machines we fund and support, like prisons and cruel rehabs, rob the victims of their dignity and leave many of them powerless to regain their agency and their lives. We are so caught up in the shame machines that we build more of them.

We can work to change course by following the dignity road map Hicks has laid out. The essence of it is to respect every other human being. This means acknowledging that they're being seen and heard, and resisting the temptation to exclude them. It means being fair to people and looking out for their safety—including safety from being shamed and humiliated. One of the most powerful ways to confer this dignity, Hicks says, is simply to give people the benefit of the doubt.

Hicks says she still struggles to live up to her ideals. We all do. Each time we look away from someone asking for money on the street, for example, or speed past a person sleeping under a bridge, we withhold respect, trust, and inclusion, not to mention any concern for the person's safety. But we also contribute to the sorry status quo by perpetuating the norms that prop up the ruling shame machines. If we accept that the fat, the poor, those with addictions, and so many others are suffering because they made bad choices, we, too, are part of the problem.

Developing awareness of the dignity violations we commit daily represents the first step toward dismantling the shame machines.

PART II

NETWORKED
SHAME

CHAPTER 5

CLICK ON CONFLICT

One day in 2012, an extremely heavy woman was reaching for a case of soda in a Missouri Walmart when her motorized cart tipped over. After she tumbled in a heap to the floor, she saw a flash of light and heard girls giggling.

To protect her from further shaming, I'll call her Joanna McCabe. A mother of two, McCabe suffered from a spinal condition known as spondylolisthesis. This made it painful to walk. She was clinically depressed and hardly surprised to find herself the object of scorn and laughter. "I thought nothing of it," she later wrote, "because I am used to hearing people make fun of me or saying snide remarks. It was nothing new."

Someone had taken her picture. It quickly found its way onto a mocking website called People of Walmart, and from there to Reddit and Facebook. Joanna McCabe went viral. In comments on social networks, people had fun with her and ridiculed her life choices. The ignorance of a fat woman reaching for soda pop! But the most damning element was the photo. With social media as a potent force accelerator, the image of a large woman splayed on the floor of a supermarket spread to a significant chunk of humanity.

McCabe fell victim to a new and potent variety of shame machines. Digital titans, led by Facebook and Google, not only profit from shame events but are engineered to exploit and diffuse them. In their massive research labs, mathematicians work closely with psychologists and anthropologists, using our behavioral data to train their machines. Their objective is to spur customer participation and to mine advertising gold. When it comes to this type of intense engagement, shame is one of the most potent motivators. It's right up there with sex. So even if the data scientists and their bosses in the executive suites might not map out a strategy based on shaming, their automatic algorithms zero in on it. It spurs traffic and boosts revenue.

You could argue that the people mocking Joanna McCabe didn't intend to hurt her. They were just having a laugh. The photo of her tumble at Walmart provided an opportunity to preen on social media and to drive up reputations, gaining likes and followers. And yes, this was largely performative shaming. However, looking at the incident through the lens of shame, the online horde was punching down on the fallen shopper to no constructive end. It was hardly an attempt to prod a wayward soul back to shared norms. For most people, she was just a digital piñata.

This is the toxic nature of shame networks, and their appeal is potent. When we express indignation in a tweet or zap some miscreant on Facebook, it makes us feel good. The reward circuits in the striatum, a section of the forebrain, light up, says Molly Crockett, a psychology researcher at Yale. It's similar to the neural feedback we get when we eat or have sex or snort a line of cocaine. Crockett says that the brain evolved to reward behaviors that propagate the species. And keeping fellow community members in line passes that test. Outrage satisfies, even if it's the product of a vile and baseless accusation.

In the pre-internet age, an embarrassing moment like a fall in the soda aisle might have generated some jokes among friends and neighbors. But today a single slip can send the networked shame machinery into overdrive, turning it into a global event.* Egged on by algorithms, millions of us participate in these dramas, providing the tech giants with free labor. The activity they market has an outsize role in defining the lives we lead and the society we create. The shame flowing through these networks affects not only the way we think but what we accept as truth.

The strange case of the so-called Covington boys is a prime example of this diverging reality. In January 2019, students from a boys' high school in northern Kentucky, Covington Catholic, had attended an antiabortion rally in Washington. They were waiting near the Lincoln Memorial for buses to take them home.

At that point, based on the first videos that emerged, one of the students, a sixteen-year-old named Nick Sandmann, had what appeared to be a confrontation with Nathan Phillips, an elder from the Omaha tribe. Phillips was chanting and beating a drum. Sandmann, wearing a red Make America Great Again cap, held his face inches from Phillips's. He appeared to be taunting him with a smirk. Then again, his look might have simply been a function of teenage awkwardness. The signal emanating from that one boy's face was ambiguous, and when the photos and video clips popped up on social media, it promptly triggered a cultural and political explosion. It started on the left, where Sandmann, wearing his Trump hat, seemed to epitomize contempt and intolerance on at least two levels. He appeared to be a privileged white male scorning an indigenous person, and also a callow youth belittling a dignified old man.

A BuzzFeed writer, Anne Helen Peterson, tweeted that Sandmann's expression was the "look of white patriarchy." David Simon,

---

* For more examples of viral and international shaming incidents, see Jon Ronson's excellent book *So You've Been Publicly Shamed*.

who created HBO's *The Wire,* said that Sandmann's hat symbolized "raw evil." Alyssa Milano, an actress, evoked the Ku Klux Klan, tweeting that the red hat was the "new white hood." Reza Aslan, author of the bestselling *Zealot: The Life and Times of Jesus of Nazareth,* summed up the animosity succinctly (in a tweet he later deleted): "Honest question. Have you ever seen a more punchable face than this kid's?"

These posts and others like them generated millions of shares and retweets. Based on a few seconds of video, a hitherto obscure high school student was infamous. He wasn't noticeably different from his peers, like a boy in Amish garb or a giant. In fact, he looked to be a typical white American high school student, an archetype of the genre. And if he had been wearing a baseball cap from one team or another, his encounter with Nathan Phillips might have gone unremarked. But the red MAGA hat he was wearing signaled to Aslan, among many others, that he was hateful, a monster, and that it might feel good to assault him.

Naturally, forces on the right commenced a counterattack. Public Advocate of the United States, a Washington policy group, praised Sandmann in a since-deleted tweet for not flinching "in the face of a berserk leftist screaming and banging his 'tribal' war drum." Fox commentator Laura Ingraham urged Twitter to shut down "sadistic online savagery" from the Left.

Over the next few weeks, other videos of the incident surfaced, providing more context. The Covington students, it turned out, had been facing angry racist heckling from a small contingent of Black Hebrew Israelites, a group that includes Black supremacists. This had led to a confrontation, in which the boys attempted to drown out the heckling with school cheers and chants.

It was at that point that Phillips walked between the two groups with his drum, attempting, he later said, to tamp down the altercation.

The details remained murky. But each side, Left and Right, found plenty of justification for their fusillades of shame. As Zack Beauchamp later wrote in *Vox,* the episode quickly turned into a social and political Rorschach test, in which each side saw the abominations of their opponents and shamed them. It devolved into a battle of memes, with the Left denouncing racism and smug white privilege, while the Right excoriated puritanical political correctness and bias against Christians and whites. Sandmann became an icon of freedom, a victim of the Left's "cancel culture." A year later, he was a featured speaker at the 2020 Republican National Convention. By that point, all hope for sifting through the nuance of his bizarre encounter in Washington, D.C., was lost.

Picture for a moment one of the millions of Americans dragged into this drama. On a January morning, still in his bathrobe, a man somewhere in America turns on his phone or laptop and sees the photo of the face-off between Nick Sandmann and Nathan Phillips. Depending on the political bubble this person inhabits, he consumes anger and indignation from one side or the other, and he's moved to participate. First he shares an angry tweet and "likes" a hard-hitting critique on Facebook. Then he composes a tweet of his own. He feels a growing sense of satisfaction as others retweet it and register likes, and it keeps him glued to his computer.

The mood shifts, though, as angry responses to his tweet pour in. They shame him for being unfair to a kid, or for being a racist, or for being a stooge of one side or the other. This upsets him. He ponders his responses. Even when he moderates his tone, trying to find some common ground, a slew of angry tweets rains down on him. His outrage grows.

Hours pass. The day is nearly gone. This person and millions of others have spent precious time broadcasting to the world the other side's misdeeds and depravity. While this day's drama commenced with the showdown near the Lincoln Memorial, it has metastasized into a shaming brawl, with people hurling grievances and accusations back and forth.

These never-ending battles not only spur traffic on social media platforms and pile up rich advertising revenue but also provide valuable data. As people stake out their positions, sharing the posts they agree with and denouncing their enemies, the platforms learn something about them. This knowledge enables them to place each user into ever more finely calibrated subgroups—which makes the targeted advertising even more effective and more profitable. The result is that shame machines such as Facebook and Google have seen their stocks skyrocket over the past decade, turning them into trillion-dollar companies, among the most valuable in the world.

For the internet titans, this windfall from conflicts isn't simply a matter of good luck. Their platforms are engineered to spur these lucrative disputes. And they tend to push users toward extreme positions, which heats up the battles, making them harder to resist.

Publishers, of course, have cashed in on conflict for centuries. In *The Man in the Red Coat,* the novelist Julian Barnes describes the state of the art in the nineteenth century: "When a newspaper's circulation begins to dip, one of the editors gets to work and writes a scathing article in which he insults one or other of his colleagues. The other answers back. The public's attention is caught; they watch as if they're in a wrestling booth at a fair."

Facebook understands the phenomenon well. In 2018, according to *The Wall Street Journal,* an internal study concluded: "Our algorithms exploit the human brain's attraction to divisiveness. If left unchecked," it cautioned, the platform would continue to host "more and more divisive content."

This is the nature of automated platforms governed by machine-learning algorithms. If the system's objective is to maximize traffic and revenue, it automatically distributes and promotes the information that leads to the most clicks, comments, and shares. And since we're much more likely to respond to threats and attacks than pleas for civil and nuanced discourse, we click on nastiness and soon find ourselves enmeshed in it.

Because of this design, social media platforms are highly successful at stoking outrage and ill-adapted, to say the least, for reaching peaceful consensus. When Facebook executives were confronted with their internal study, which raised uncomfortable moral questions about their business model, they shelved the research, according to *The Wall Street Journal*. Later, in 2020, a civil rights audit commissioned by Facebook itself charged that the company's leadership was not "sufficiently attuned to the depth of concern on the issue of polarization and the way that the algorithms used by Facebook inadvertently fuel extreme and polarizing content." The auditors added that neglecting to address this issue could "have dangerous (and life-threatening) real-world consequences." If they were looking for evidence, it came less than a year later when an angry mob, nourished by conspiracy theories proliferating on social media platforms, invaded the Capitol in Washington, sowing death and destruction and threatening to hang the vice president of the United States.

You would think that a traumatic event like that might have forged at least a semblance of horrified unity, perhaps similar to the public response following the terror attacks of September 11, 2001. But those strikes were unleashed before the birth of online social networks. In the following decades, the digital juggernauts accelerated the fracturing of public opinion into tiny and isolated groups that all too often fail to understand or respect one another.

The trouble with our new cohorts, both online and in social gatherings, is that it's increasingly hard to see beyond them. They tend to dominate our information channels and mold our worldview. The result is that many of us can be fooled into believing the values that we share with our like-minded friends are universal.

We've made so much progress, we think to ourselves. But who is "we"?

In many college settings, for example, it is close to axiomatic that caring people should list their pronouns with their contact details and use the latest approved terminology and acronyms for different races, ethnicities, and gender identities. From this perspective, steady progress has been "achieved" in recent years in confronting historical injustices, and this new vocabulary reflects those reckonings. In this way, our language sprouts new norms, and those who stick with the old words need a course correction. Sometimes the prompt comes from a dose of shame, whether a scolding in a classroom or a video of someone's faux pas posted on social media.

The trouble is that what appears to one community as accepted truth, achieved through long and thorough discussion, remains utterly foreign to those in another group. It's as if they missed the memo. Pronouns? Why? Does that mean I'm insulting people if I don't display mine? Instead of seeing these language tweaks as the reasonable conclusions of a conversation around justice, they instead represent baffling new mandates created by a sanctimonious tribe of aliens, in this case, the "woke." So the two sides shame each other, one for propagating new orthodoxies and the other for rejecting them.

Blinkered inside our small online contingents, dialogue shrivels and misunderstanding grows, along with contempt. As a result, we tend to see others not just as different but as followers of cults. They often think the same about us.

Let's say you open Facebook and see an alert. You click, and to your horror you see that someone has posted a group picture and *tagged* you. It turns out to be terribly unflattering, perhaps the ugliest picture of you imaginable. And your name pops up for all to see when the cursor passes over your image. That tag is nefarious, because it means that whenever anyone searches the internet for you or anyone else tagged in that photo, or for that matter anything related to the event you were attending, that cringeworthy image will show up. It sticks to your identity and is dragged along, like a piece of toilet paper on a shoe.

The misery we inflict on others via digital shame machines, often without knowing it, accounts for only the most obvious grief. The more pervasive abuses are engineered to whir away on their own. And this automated poison is progressing at such a furious pace that science fiction from only a few years ago now reads like today's news. Gary Shteyngart's 2010 novel, *Super Sad True Love Story*, for example, describes a futuristic world in which radically open data is the norm, and the possibility of shaming lurks around every corner. Credit scores appear on a public display when characters walk past a "credit pole" in the neighborhood. The advanced cellphones, or äppäräts, can scan the net worth and financial history of each passerby. If someone in a bar tells a joke that falls flat, their "hotness" and "personality" scores plummet in real time.

Abuses very much like these are already spreading, especially in China, where state surveillance operates without even a hint of restraint. There are constellations of government-sanctioned social credit scores, some of which ding a given person if a surveillance camera catches them lighting up in a no-smoking zone or playing too many videogames. Others use cameras equipped with AI that can identify individuals based on a combination of facial features, posture, and gait. So if, say, someone is heading to work and gets caught jaywalking, the smart cam can tag the name and personal information of the offender and flash it across a digital billboard. Or likewise you might get punished for littering in the subway or denigrating the ruling party online. Your various infractions might also be announced, by name, on Weibo or WeChat, internet giants in China.

No matter where we live, some of us fare far better than others in our relations with the expanding network linking data to shame and stigma. The easiest people to exploit tend to be the most desperate, the ones who lack the money, the knowledge, or the leisure time to tend to the digital baggage that trails them, or simply those who have traditionally been treated badly. These are folks who are disproportionately poor or otherwise marginalized and have the least control over their identities. We've already seen how their lives are defined, and poisoned, by shame machines: the diet industry, opioid merchants, for-profit prisons, welfare bureaucracies, and rehab centers that harvest their unpaid labor. Those machines punch down on them relentlessly.

But shame has a second life in the data economy. Evictions, brushes with child protective services or the law, trips to casinos—all leave rich trails of information, creating a bonanza for the many institutions that feed on shame data. These stretch far beyond the social networks, to the formal economy of credit rating companies, mortgage brokers, and parole boards, as well as a vast who's who of hucksters and scam artists. The episodes that trigger the most shame are digitized, codified, and then processed by hundreds or thousands of different algorithms to size up the people involved, make money from them, and deprive them of opportunities, often permanently.

This is very much like the red *A* for adultery that Hester Prynne was sentenced to wear in Hawthorne's *Scarlet Letter*. But in this modern incarnation, the stigma is digital. No longer pinned to a dress, in the Puritan tradition, it endures as myriad risk scores in the mammoth data centers stored in computer clouds.

Wiping these digital scarlet letters clean is no simple matter. While it's true that the criminal justice system in the United States enables people who have been cleared of a crime to expunge the charge from their official records, the mugshots and charges persist on the internet and show up in search engine results. One New Jersey man named Alan was charged in 2017 with a crime resulting from a misunderstanding: A summons to appear in municipal court had been sent to the wrong address. The judge understood this and promptly vacated the charge. Yet Alan, as described in *Slate*, struggled mightily to remove his (false) arrest record from the internet. After contacting lots of website administrators and the state police, he had limited success. But all the while, he kept receiving come-ons from "reputation management" consultants, who offered to erase his mugshots for a fee. The vast economic ecosystem of digital shame offers endless opportunities to make a buck.

On a wintry afternoon in New York, I'm sitting with a group of young women. They're seniors at an elite private school in the city. (For their privacy, I've agreed to shield their names and school.) By most standards, they lead charmed lives, among the very best the twenty-first century can provide. If they struggle with math, they get tutored. If their faces break out, the dermatologist is on call. Their parents will spend whatever it takes to help them hoist their college board scores to where they should be. Money is no constraint. At this point—halfway through their senior year—most of them have already been accepted into the most prestigious colleges and universities in the country. That huge hurdle is behind them. In a society plagued by inequality, they're on the winning side.

And yet, when I bring up the subject of shame, it's as if I've lifted the lid from a boiling cauldron. Stories about humiliation and nightmarish rankings spill out. A girl might be slut-shamed after a party, do badly on a test, or be fat-shamed on Instagram by the group of girls she had hoped to be friends with. In comparison to the torrents of shame that pound the poor, the addicted, or the incarcerated, these concerns are tame, even frivolous. But they are all too real to these students. Even in their world of privilege, they experience torment. One of them describes the shame she felt when she disappointed a college track coach. "I was supposed to tell the coach that I'd run a 5:10, and my time was 5:20:7. I was ten seconds off, and thirty points behind the target in the SATs," she says. "I felt so imperfect."

The digital world amps up these competitions at every step. Social media serves as jury and judge, and scrutinizes the competitors 24/7. Successes are indelibly registered, available at a click. So are failures. And each stumble is recorded, potentially shared, and retrievable forever.

This creates pressure, which is already intense among high school students. For the young women I talked to, every Instagram post is a roll of the dice. They detailed for me the analysis they sometimes carry out to make sure that each photo delivers a meticulously honed message, with the body shown in the most flattering pose, no fat hanging over the belt, no trace of zit cream on the forehead. Their Instagram dramas are similar to age-old quandaries about what girls would wear to a high school dance or the beach or, a century ago, the ball. The difference now is that they're preening—and vulnerable—on a global network.

This hypervisibility can reinforce cycles of shame. One of the students I talked to, for example, told me she was "obsessive" about her eating in the ninth grade. "I would feel terrible if I had an ice cream," she says. The fixation mounted, and the list of forbidden foods grew. Pretty soon, she wasn't eating much at all, and was losing lots of weight.

Such eating disorders, of course, existed long before the internet. But the dynamics of the social networks can add dangerous new elements. This student, for example, got therapy and started eating normally. She gained back much of the weight. But now, as she flips through hundreds of photos of herself, looking for the right ones to post on Instagram, she finds herself admiring her shots from ninth grade—when she was starving herself. If she posts those pictures, propagating a thinner version of herself in the networked world, it could create an embarrassing disconnect between her online image and the one people see at school. And that could lead a young person to bring the two into sync—and relapse into dangerous dieting.

The relentless pressure to optimize appearances on social networks—and the unfathomable reservoir of opportunities to self-criticize—has spawned an entire ecosystem of body-editing apps. Those ashamed of their straight or frizzy hair, the shape of their eyes, or the tone of their skin can make adjustments. But for many teenagers, the body itself is most urgently in need of a fix. Bodytune is one of many apps that make it easy for women to expand their bust, slim their waist, and widen their hips. With a couple of clicks, they can elongate legs or harden a soft stomach into washboard abs. It lets them create a version of themselves that they can be proud of. It bills itself as the app "everyone is secretly using."

One reviewer on the App Store, who calls herself BarbieLoves-Billy, raves: "This app really helps flaunt what God gave you without other social media users seeing your edited pic and immediately thinking PHOTOSHOP!" But she complains that these editing apps are getting "greedy." Bodytune bills users a $29.99 annual fee after a three-day trial. Unless you're "boocoo rich," she warns, "this app will leave you broke."

The key, whether it's plastic surgery or a smartphone app, is to make it look natural, as though the person *deserves* to look so wonderful. Shortcuts, like photo editing in the digital realm or plastic surgery in the physical one, are seen as cheating, which in turn generates more shame. It's like applying for welfare instead of a job, or battling an opioid addiction with methadone instead of sucking it up and going cold turkey.

All of these networked behaviors, from sharing Bodytune swimsuit shots to sending out righteous tweets, fuel falsehoods and delusions. They are focused on redefining the world—and channeling shame from ourselves onto others. And because entire online communities affirm them with likes, shares, and emojis, they can be seductively easy to believe. Yes, you're beautiful, the crowd responds to a doctored selfie. Others are ugly, even hideous. And when you gleefully share a photo of a fallen fat woman in the aisle of Walmart, they affirm your virtue. You're just giving her a helpful nudge to improve her health. This is fiction, of course, poison masquerading as spring water. Sadly, the damage extends far beyond individuals.

The shame networks are busy engaging us to rip apart our social fabric, and in doing so, addict us to the short-term highs, the feelings of petty power or outrage or vengeance. And so we will continue on, living in ever-smaller communities that we feel are looking out for us, focused on our outsize emotions instead of the poorly designed system that provokes them automatically. It's a perpetual shame machine.

CHAPTER 6

HUMILIATION AND DEFIANCE

O n a sunny Memorial Day in 2020, a forty-year-old financial analyst named Amy Cooper took her cocker span-
iel, Henry, for a walk in New York City's Central Park.
She unleashed the dog in a wild part of the park known as the
Ramble. A nature preserve, the Ramble is popular among birders.
And when one of them asked Amy Cooper to leash her dog, she
refused. This sparked a racial incident that soon spread across the
internet.

The birder was a fifty-seven-year-old man named Christian
Cooper, no relation to the dog walker. He hardly fit the descriptive
stereotype of a threatening man. He wore binoculars around his
neck and carried a birding guide. He had a soft voice and emphasized the word "please" when asking Amy Cooper not to unleash
Henry. Yet despite his gentle mien and establishment credentials,
including a degree from Harvard and membership on the board of
the New York City Audubon Society, Christian Cooper had one
threatening trait: he was Black. Amy Cooper said she felt unsettled
and called the police. The birder pulled his smartphone from his
pocket and recorded as she falsely reported that an African American man had attacked her.

Later that day, Christian Cooper posted the video on Facebook,
along with his recollection of the dialogue that took place before

Amy Cooper called the police. In this description, he referred to her as a "Karen."

The Karen meme, barely two years old at the time, refers to white women who exercise their privilege and power over Black people by appealing to higher authorities, whether a store manager or the cops. In 2018, a so-called Karen in Oakland, California, was recorded alerting police to what she believed was a Black family's illegal charcoal barbecue in a park. She became known as "BBQ Becky." In June 2020, in the liberal New Jersey suburb of Montclair, a woman named Susan Schulz dialed 911 to report that her Black neighbors were building a patio without a permit. She became known as "Permit Karen."

To be deemed a Karen, and to have your moment of white privilege blasted across the internet, is to undergo intense and widespread shaming. Within hours of Susan Schulz's call to the police, dozens of neighbors and activists in Montclair were demonstrating outside her home, chanting and holding signs that read NOT HERE!, BLACK LIVES MATTER, and WHITE ENTITLEMENT IS VIOLENCE.

Amy Cooper, the Central Park dog walker, faced a much larger wave of shaming on TV and social media. She issued a contrite apology. But it was too late. The following day her employer, Franklin Templeton, fired her, effective immediately.* "We do not tolerate racism of any kind at Franklin Templeton," the company tweeted. Association with a Karen, it seemed, could tarnish the reputation of an entire enterprise.

This is a new flavor of shame. Just a few years ago, a white woman reporting a supposedly threatening Black man to the police might not have experienced any pushback whatsoever. In fact, she might have gotten sympathy from the cops, and even appreciation for

---

* As of this writing, she is suing her former employer on the grounds that they discriminated against her on the basis of her race and gender.

alerting them to a potential problem. Within her cohort, the suggestion that she was a racist might have seemed outlandish. That was her uncle, who dropped the N-word at Thanksgiving dinner, or the Minneapolis cop, Derek Chauvin, who clamped his knee on the neck of George Floyd and suffocated him—on the very same day as the Central Park bird-watching incident, as it happens. Those people were racists. But a person reporting a threatening man? In the past, that was seen as acceptable behavior.* Yet now, thanks to changing norms, that same behavior turns her into a monster, with shame leveled at her from around the world.

Networked shame engines stoke these conflicts and accelerate their spread. With today's instantaneous communication, people have less time to catch up to the new standards and adjust their beliefs and behaviors. This produces intense unhappiness and social friction. As you might expect, shame fuels this discomfort. It's the force pushing people to adapt to society's expectations.

Historically, shifts like these have happened gradually. During much of the twentieth century, for example, it was common in many workplaces to make fun of gay people and to shun them. Homophobia was mainstream. However, as more people came out, showing themselves to be sons and daughters and colleagues, more and more communities and industries started to frown upon open homophobia. It wasn't tolerated anymore. It was hateful. The norm changed. In many quarters, it was homophobia that became shameful, not homosexuality. This evolution extended throughout the economy, with industries like fashion and entertainment leading the way, and gradually spread to the mainstream.

For those who haven't adapted to new norms, these changes can be jarring. A natural response to a viral wave of shaming is anger

---

*Recall, if you will the 2014 app SketchFactor that positively encouraged such reporting.

and indignation. It is here that people enter the second stage of shame, denial.

One hallmark of this stage is cognitive dissonance. I'm not a bad person, Permit Karen might think. And yet people are outside my door raging at me. I'm not a racist, and yet my community insists that I am one. I must deny it.

Cognitive dissonance—holding two ideas that appear to contradict each other—can cause great emotional stress and lead to tortured logic. The term was minted in the 1950s by a social psychologist at the University of Minnesota, Leon Festinger, and two colleagues. They studied a cult that was convinced that a flood would drown humanity on December 21, 1954. The cult leader, a Chicagoan named Dorothy Martin, promised her followers that aliens would rescue them and zip them away in flying saucers before the waters rose too high. The aliens, of course, never arrived. Nor did the flood.

The psychologists found that fringe members of the cult had little trouble adjusting their convictions. They hadn't been deeply invested in the prophecy, and, yes, they'd been fools to buy into it. They avoided cognitive dissonance by letting go of beliefs that they saw were demonstrably false. Those who had assured friends and family that the end was at hand must have endured ridicule and shame.

The most committed cultists, however, took a different tack. They created a scenario in which their contradictory views could coexist. Yes, the flood had been coming, they insisted. And the aliens had been ready to whisk them away. But it was the steadfast action of their community, and the strength of its members' beliefs, that had saved humanity from a watery end. The cult didn't shrivel, as many had expected; instead, it grew.

A similar dilemma confronts people like the Karens, who view themselves as victims of fast-changing norms. Their choice is to adjust to the new order, adopting new terminology and behaviors, or, conversely, to question the premise of the attack. A common course is to denigrate the shamers and reject their verdict, or even to create an alternate reality, one that feels better.

We'll see this time and again as we explore the fast-shifting beliefs and strictures of our time. The rules change. As the Karens can attest, vivid and shareable video of how people behave can reach a merciless jury of millions within an hour or two. This process is turbocharged by the social media platforms, which are the richest and most prodigious shame engines ever devised. The judgments they transmit trigger a host of reactions: pain, fury, denial, and often a frantic search for acceptance and community. And this gives birth to splinter groups and cults that reject mainstream views, choosing instead to piece together their own narratives and often conjuring up their own facts.

Despite their optimizing algorithms, however, the platforms need help to manufacture shame. That's where we come in. Hundreds of millions of us summon the requisite outrage and censure, often convincing ourselves that these microdoses of shame nudge the world toward justice and equality. After all, that's what shame is for, isn't it? The idea has always been to sting outliers, shepherding them back to shared values and acceptable behavior. A white woman calling a cop to settle a dispute with a Black neighbor is *not* OK, and she should be punished.

But think back to the Pueblo shame clowns. They were using comedy and shame to deliver lessons to members of their community, people they cared about and would check up on. Compare that to the vindictive social media posts denouncing Montclair's Susan Schulz, aka Permit Karen. One liberal Twitter user, Miz-FlagPin, states on her profile that "Together we stand for Truth, Justice, and the American Way." Yet responding to Schulz's videoed run-in with her neighbors, MizFlagPin tweeted that Schulz's case, on the basis of a single video, was effectively closed: "She's been identified. The neighbors she harassed are lawyers. Neighborhood youth protested outside her home. Neighbors sided with the lawyers. Stick a fork in her. She's done." It seemed like her objective was to banish Schulz from the community, not to help her adapt to new guidelines. For all I know, MizFlagPin and others denouncing Susan Schulz on social media may devote themselves to advancing the cause of racial justice. But much of the traffic around these incidents, it's safe to say, is performative. People are signaling virtue and shared values to their friends and followers, and building their personal brand, to gain more followers and to feel righteous. This does little else but fuel relentless traffic and increase profits for social media platforms.

One consequence of this never-ending optimization of these shame networks is the rapid growth of the so-called cancel culture. Feeding on tweets, YouTube videos, and Instagram posts, it's like an enormous village council that judges people for their behavior, whether in words or actions. The Karens are prominent targets, or victims. And you can easily make a case that the attacks on them serve a social function. Perhaps at this very moment a white person is arguing with a Black neighbor. Recalling a much-publicized Karen scandal, he or she is resisting the temptation to call the cops. In that sense, mass shaming can prod society along a healthier path.

At the same time, torrents of networked shame raining down on an individual raise basic questions about crime and punishment. Does any woman deserve to bear a digital scarlet letter for the rest of her days simply because she acted foolishly one summer afternoon? Should she lose her job? These are key questions for fairness. But they're also central to strategy, because the shame weaponized in these online pile-ons can spark angry countermovements. Their excesses, often exaggerated, also provide a handy defense for powerful people under attack, who can then position themselves as victims of a hypersensitive elite. In early 2021, when numerous women accused New York's Democratic governor, Andrew Cuomo, of sexual harassment, he vowed that he would not resign, as that would be "bowing to cancel culture." And with that, he managed to avoid scrutiny, at least for some months. When a blistering report by New York's attorney general, Letitia James, made it clear that the charges were serious, far beyond any fabrications of cancel culture, Cuomo resigned, while still refusing to admit that he'd done wrong.

Conservatives in growing numbers, meanwhile, cite the most egregious cases, some real, others fictitious, to demonize the Left as a punishing horde of thought police, just a step or two away from the ruthless overseers of Mao Zedong's Cultural Revolution. At the same time, they eagerly cancel people themselves. For example, they hounded San Francisco 49ers quarterback Colin Kaepernick out of the National Football League after he spearheaded a peaceful movement in 2016 to protest police brutality against Black people.

Canceling people in the modern sense is akin to religious shunning: refusing to talk or even look at a former friend or neighbor who has left the faith. It can come with the best of intentions—to banish racism from our society, to respect women, or to defend the rights of people to assert their gender identity. In many ways, though, the process can resemble a crowdsourced criminal investigation. Amateur sleuths sift through backlogs of social media postings—or they train software to do the job. And if they find evidence of bad behavior, whether in word or deed, they can raise armies of followers to target the offenders, eventually getting them fired or deposed, and stigmatizing them for a lifetime.

If you look at cancel culture from the perspective of Donna Hicks, it's bristling with dignity violations. It does not seek out dialogue and understanding, or provide a hearing for the accused.

Instead it demands a groveling apology, which often brings the target precious little relief. Amplified by optimizing algorithms of the internet giants, this process enforces rules, often punishing people for a single misdeed and denying them due process. Hicks, by contrast, encourages people to give others the benefit of the doubt.

The other reason to check our shaming impulse is that virtuous tweetstorms often leave the underlying issues untouched. People who experience a twinge of guilt about moving from the city to a rich white suburb for its good schools might feel ennobled by sharing on Instagram a video of a Karen caught in the act, and packaging it with a biting put-down. While this may be satisfying, it sets too low a bar for anti-racist creds. It's much harder—but more necessary—to desegregate schools, open up zoning, and extend economic opportunities. Focusing on Karen episodes "lets white people off the hook," wrote Christian Cooper, the Central Park bird-watcher in a *Washington Post* op-ed. "They can scream for her head while leaving their own prejudices unexamined."

Giving in to online rage can also trigger what is now known as "white fragility." In that state, white people feel so offended by the suggestion that they hold any responsibility for racism that they see themselves as aggrieved victims. Instead of confronting their shame, their cognitive dissonance forces them to repress potentially painful probes into racism and instead ask a simple question: Am I a good person? An affirmative answer provides a measure of emotional peace, but it's a fragile one, because of all those unanswered questions about race, and the doubts they stir.

We saw this play out in the anti-racism uprising in the summer of 2020. Largely peaceful protests erupted in much of the country, some of them marred by vandalism performed by a tiny minority of those in attendance. Defenders of the police, including the president, focused on the violence, accused the protesters of terrorism and hate crimes, and called in the army to quell them. This was the government and its supporters in denial, the second stage of shame. They were basking in an alternative narrative, one that minimized both the destructive force of racism and their role in sustaining it.

It follows a pattern that has marked race relations in this country since the first enslaved Africans landed in 1619. Oppressors experience shame, some to a greater extent than others. So they find it much more comfortable to deny the human rights abuses they're benefiting from and to rally instead around myths.* In the nineteenth century, for example, the bogus science of phrenology—which correlated human abilities to the shape and contours of the skull—bolstered the agenda of white supremacists. Similar flimsy arguments masquerading as science shifted their focus, a century later, from the skull to the genome.

Many of those who still venerate the Confederate flag take refuge in false and self-flattering versions of history. If slavery was a crime against humanity, then the role the South played was morally depraved, and that's unfathomable. The Stars and Bars crowd has good reason to come up with prettier stories, in order to quell its cognitive dissonance.

Lots of the fiction made it into textbooks, indoctrinating entire generations with the mythology of the South's Lost Cause. Well into the 1970s, schoolbooks in many states not only avoided mention of the brutality of slavery but emphasized instead the supposedly loving relations on plantations. Writing in *The Washington Post*, Bennett Minton, a Virginian, revisited a textbook assigned to his seventh-grade class: *Virginia: History, Government, Geography.*

---

*This starts, of course, with racist ideas themselves. See Ibram X. Kendi's *Stamped from the Beginning* for a historical treatment.

One chapter, "How the Negroes Lived under Slavery," declared: "A feeling of strong affection existed between masters and slaves in a majority of Virginia homes."

The whitewashing continued: "Some of the Negro servants left the plantations because they heard President Lincoln was going to set them free. But most of the Negroes stayed on the plantations and went on with their work. Some of them risked their lives to protect the white people they loved." And Confederate icons were lauded: "General Lee was a handsome man with a kind, strong face. He sat straight and firm in his saddle. Traveller [his horse] stepped proudly as if he knew that he carried a great general."

That self-serving narrative has, happily, been challenged of late. As the nation turned its attention to racial injustice, activists tore down statues of Confederate icons. The once-sterling reputation of General Lee took a hit. A growing number of people no longer regarded him as the noble hero of a mythical Lost Cause, but as a traitor who waged war against the United States to keep millions enslaved. And the Confederate flag, long an emblem of regional pride, was increasingly seen as a rallying symbol of racial hatred, which had fueled a century and a half of injustice and unspeakable violence, including thousands of Ku Klux Klan lynchings. As norms changed, the Confederate flag assumed its place as an American cousin of the Nazi swastika. Even Mississippi removed its image from the state flag.

This new norm shames millions of Americans who read those textbooks and still cling to that false but comforting version of history. Most of them do not consider themselves racist, much less traitors to the United States.

They're firmly locked into anger and denial. It provides bottomless opportunity for race-baiting politicians, who appeal to shared grievances. Those new "woke" orthodoxies about race are misguided, they tell voters. *You're good. Your myths are true. It's the people shaming you who are bad.* This feeds the absurd contention, supremely consoling for many, that white people are the victims, not the perpetrators, of racism. Such an approach bypasses the necessary hard work, the much-needed reflection and dialogue on race, the reckoning. Instead it substitutes a simple and easy route to unalloyed hatred. The only chance for racial peace and progress on this front, says Eddie S. Glaude Jr., a professor of African American studies at Princeton, is "to convince white folks to . . . embrace a history that might set them free from being white."

The range of white shame is extraordinarily broad. On one side, millions of whites have joined the protests against police brutality and racial injustice. They are facing facts and finding solidarity with citizens of all colors. They've moved past the denial stage of shame into acceptance, even transcendence.*

At the other end of the spectrum, we have white nationalists burrowing ever deeper into their synthetic narrative, which wraps them in a cocoon of denial. Looking at it from their point of view, it might seem that much of the country is turning against them as white men. During the months of Black Lives Matter marches in the summer of 2020, even the titans of the Dow 30, from airlines to pharmaceutical giants, rushed to produce TV spots denouncing systemic racism. Since then, though, the battle over a racial reckoning among white people continues, including a proposed law in Tennessee to make it illegal to talk about systemic racism in educational settings.

This mainstreaming of the issue has made it ever harder for the deniers to avoid. The process of abandoning cozy and well-worn stories is uncomfortable, and should be. It's how we as a society drag people, kicking and screaming, to the unwelcome truth. It's a tough transition. But why bother with it if you can escape, with a

---

*At least for police violence. We are still waiting on zoning laws and schools.

mouse click or a tap on the remote, into narratives absolving you of all shame?

I have a formative memory from junior high school, when I suppose I started thinking about the denial stage of white shame (although I certainly wouldn't have called it that at the time). My history teacher was describing Manifest Destiny, the driving vision of the nineteenth century, which held that white European Protestants would settle the entire continent, from Atlantic to Pacific, and exercise their dominion. By late in the twentieth century, my classmates and I could see that it was a naked land grab and justification for the genocide of Native Americans.

It was a creation story, but looking forward instead of back. It provided divine justification for killing fellow human beings for their property. It made white settlers feel better about themselves, washing away a great deal of the shame of raping and pillaging. But it didn't always work. People have consciences. Hollywood, according to the French philosopher René Girard, came up with a formula to absolve white settlers of genocide. For decades, he writes, movies framed the drama around survival: The Indian must die to save the whole (white) nation. In these cases, Girard writes, "scapegoating must remain unconscious, [so that] the operation of transferring sins from the community to the victim seemed to occur from beyond, without [the whites'] own real participation."

Like many others, I vacillated between feeling shame as a white beneficiary of these crimes and putting them at arm's length, halfway between paying attention and trying to tune it out. It was deeply troubling. And I found a refuge for such feelings in mathematics. Math was just numbers; its ideas felt shame-free.

White shame stirs anxiety, not least among liberals. Sometimes this can turn ugly, as happened not long ago on New York's Upper West Side. This is a privileged swath of Manhattan, stretching north from the arts cluster around Lincoln Center to Columbia University and Barnard College, a couple of blocks from where I used to live. People there pride themselves on their openness to diversity and equality. Many of them shudder at the idea of life in a more conservative part of the country, like Texas. They often associate the diverse millions in such places with racism and intolerance.

When the COVID-19 crisis exploded in New York, in March 2020, this neighborhood became a surprising laboratory of shame. The drama started when the mayor sent several hundred homeless men to a luxury hotel, the Lucerne. The idea was to keep them safe and socially distanced during the health crisis. The landmark building, erected in 1904, had recently undergone a multimillion-dollar renovation. It was conveniently located on prime real estate for the wealthy, between the Seventy-ninth Street subway stop on Broadway and Central Park.

For thousands of local residents, their new neighbors at the Lucerne were the wrong kind of people and, most emphatically, unwelcome. On a neighborhood Facebook group, some Upper West Siders fantasized about an armed movement to expel the newcomers, whom they referred to as "scum" and "thugs." They complained about the homeless defecating on the streets and insinuated that they were infecting the neighborhood with the virus. One man suggested "having round the clock militias shooting these assholes."

One woman posting on the group, a sixty-year-old, seemed to fit the bleeding-heart liberal stereotype of the Upper West Side. (To avoid shaming her by name, I'll call her Roberta.) She served on the board of Community in Crisis, a New Jersey–based non-profit that fights the opioid epidemic and is dedicated to reducing the taboo around addiction. As she wrote in a Facebook fundraising post, her organization works to remove that stigma, to treat people with addictions simply as worthy human beings who are struggling with a serious medical issue, and to help them. Yet on the Upper West Side Facebook page, where neighbors were discussing how to keep the homeless at bay, she wrote: "Forget pepper spray or mace. Use Hornet Spray and shoot at the eyes."

Later, when contacted by a reporter for *Gothamist,* Roberta clarified that the spray should be used only in self-defense. She affirmed that she was "definitely of the Black Lives Matter Movement," and that systemic racism was a real problem—but that the decision to move the homeless into her neighborhood was a mistake.

Now, let's dig through the various flavors of shame produced by that single case. First, for Roberta, that phone call from *Gothamist* had to deliver a sudden and painful dose of it. After all, punishing the poor and downtrodden isn't her style. Unlike most of us, she's actively working to help people, in her case, those suffering with addiction.

What a nasty shock it must have been when she answered the phone one day and a reporter was asking her—for publication!—why she recommended shooting hornet spray into the eyes of poor, largely Black and Brown people. During a nightmarish pandemic, they'd had a solitary stroke of good fortune, moving from the streets and shelters into a safe and comfortable hotel. She not only wanted them gone. She also seemed prepared to hurt them, and urged her Facebook friends to follow her lead. It made her look like a cruel person, and a racist—uncomfortably close to a "Karen." That's why Roberta hastened to add that she was on board with Black Lives Matter.

She went on to detail the rationale behind the hornet spray suggestion. She was directing the advice to fellow Upper West Siders, only in the event that they were accosted by one of the homeless and had to protect themselves.

In her own account of her motivation, she claimed that her issue was not that these newcomers were poor and homeless, much less that they were one race or another. Instead it was their behavior, she argued, which was filthy and scary. They were the ones harassing people and fouling the sidewalks. So they were the guilty party. She and the others in her Facebook group were victims.

The problems she cited were real. Some of the newcomers had used the sidewalks as a toilet, and the inhabitants had not appreciated it. Yet these difficulties were caused, very likely, by just a handful of the people lodged at the hotel. They probably struggled with addiction or mental health and needed help, not hornet spray. Further, most of the other new guests at the hotel were simply living their lives, some of them working as janitors, couriers, or night guards for minimum wage, and grateful to come home to their own safe space. But the angry Facebook group treated the entire cohort as a dirty, dangerous, and unwanted presence. In doing so, they shamed the homeless and punched down on them.[*]

The shame doesn't end there. By describing these residents and their Facebook page, and citing two or three of their nastiest comments, I'm participating in this drama, along with the reporter at *Gothamist*. We are exposing them as racists, or at the very least, people engaging in racist behavior. Being called a racist on the Upper West Side risks enduring stigma.

For that matter, you could say I'm punching down on Roberta, since here I am writing about her mistakes once again and publishing them for a global audience. She has already been shamed by name. By piling on here, in this book—a commercial venture—you

---

[*] I should add here that an opposing contingent, the Upper West Side Homeless Advocacy Group, organized to defend the homeless population and resist the city's push to move them to a Radisson in the Financial District, where there were fewer busybody neighbors to upset. It was a two-way tussle.

could make the case that I am feeding and profiting from the shame machine.*

But I am doing so in hopes that we can all learn from it: As we make our way through life, most of us are likely to participate in shaming events, often without noticing. And if we're ever called to answer for the pain we deliver, we often react with bewilderment and experience cognitive dissonance. We think we're good, while the world informs us that we're not. My former neighbors on the Upper West Side could very well have believed that they were punching up at the mayor, while in fact they were punching down, some of them brutally, on the most unfortunate New Yorkers.

Much of this bafflement comes from wishful thinking. Following the massive 2020 protests against police brutality, for example, countless lawn signs sprouted in large American cities and their close suburbs. Most pledged allegiance to Black Lives Matter. Others listed a progressive catechism, avowing support for immigrants, science, feminism, the LGBTQ community, and so on.

Many of the people posting those signs no doubt felt that they had "passed" the racism test. They never used improper language. They voted for candidates committed to equality. Many went out into the streets and marched following the police murder of George Floyd in Minneapolis.

Given those post-racial credentials, it seemed safe to assume that they had overcome raw racism and moved past the performative victimhood of white fragility. Having acknowledged America's race problems, these progressive urbanites appeared to have reached the acceptance stage. And you could argue that in going out to march, some had advanced further, into transcendence. They

---

*For that matter, when companies fire their workers for mistakes they made that went viral on social media, that's also punching down, often in the guise of punching up.

were taking on the structures that sustained racial inequality. Morally, they seemed to be on firm ground.

But most of the liberals who took to the streets do not have homeless people wandering around their neighborhood, some of them using it for a toilet. They haven't been tested like Roberta. Many of them also move to prime public school districts, or send their kids to private schools, because the city schools aren't so great, certainly not good enough for their families. They sit on zoning boards to prevent affordable housing developments from being established in their neighborhoods. Some, in the guise of defending educational quality, push to preserve de facto segregation of schools. Nonetheless, they view themselves as enlightened on race.

It's not just them, of course. It's all of us. We tend to go easy on ourselves, because confronting our weaknesses is hard work. Many of us mean well. And often that seems to suffice. Yet when the real tests come, we fall short of our own standards. If we look at our lives—each relationship, each encounter—through the lens of shame, we can begin to recognize offhand remarks and even jokes as conveyors of shame. Each one of us is engaged with it, receiving and dishing it out in many different forms. Once we open our eyes to it, it's everywhere. It's making a tart comment to the intern, or instructing the grandfather, with thinly veiled contempt, how to work the TV remote. It's telling the twelve-year-old to stop eating so much dessert. It's retweeting a snarky review. The shame is not always bad or uncalled for, but it's crucial to be aware of it, especially when it happens on the lightning-fast shame networks.

In each dimension of shame, whether the issue is obesity, poverty, addiction, racism, or the struggle to achieve, each of us faces choices. Many take a stand in one area, really working at it, while utterly relaxing in another. In a single afternoon, someone might bravely face down club-wielding policemen in a march for racial justice and then take a break to send out a flurry of poisonous punching-down tweets. When it comes to shame, we can be simultaneously gentle and merciless, fighting against one stigma while defending another.

It sounds simple when you say it: Be nice. Don't spread poison. Give people the benefit of the doubt. The trouble is that we humans are prone to fooling ourselves, at times underestimating our own agency, or seeing ourselves as victims, when we're really not.

Bret Stephens, a conservative columnist for *The New York Times,* provides a pungent example of such delusion. Stephens enjoys clout that other writers and political thinkers only dream of. He can write about anything he wants on prime media real estate—the op-ed page of the world's most influential newspaper. If he levels his editorial guns at someone, they feel it.

In April 2019, it was reported that *The New York Times,* in its fifty-two-story Renzo Piano–designed headquarters in Midtown Manhattan, was struggling with a bedbug infestation. This led David Karpf, a professor of media and public affairs at George Washington University, to post on Twitter what he later called "a milquetoast joke": "The bedbugs are a metaphor. The bedbugs are Bret Stephens."

In the media balance of power, the professor had launched a solitary attack on an imposing mainstream battleship with the internet equivalent of a peashooter. Karpf's tweets reached only a handful of Twitter followers, and his joke about bedbugs, like most tweets, went largely unliked, unnoticed, un-retweeted. It seemed consigned to oblivion.

But someone showed it to Stephens, and it struck a nerve. The columnist felt victimized. It didn't matter to him that the joke reached almost no one. Stephens went on the attack. He promptly emailed Karpf and he made sure to copy the provost of Karpf's university. This was a warning shot, raising the possibility that the professor's job might be at stake. In the email, Stephens accused Karpf of a gross insult and incivility. He dared him to come to his home, where he could call the columnist a bedbug in front of Stephens's wife and children. From his heights, the columnist was shaming the professor for making a joke about him. On MSNBC, Stephens called Karpf's tweet "dehumanizing and totally unacceptable." That is to say that one obscure tweet by a little-known professor had the awesome capacity to whittle away at the columnist's humanity. This was delusion on a grand scale.*

Several days later, Stephens detailed his pain in a column reaching millions of readers. Without naming Karpf or mentioning the tweet, he tied it into a World War II narrative featuring a once-civil society falling into hatred, violence, authoritarianism, and, ultimately, genocide. "The political mind-set" of the Nazis, Stephens wrote, "that turned human beings into categories, classes and races also turned them into rodents, insects and garbage." Karpf's tweet, though small, was an example of a poisonous trend, one that could lead our country to disaster.

Stephens, to be fair, made some good points. It is true, as we've seen, that social media empowers online posses that can victimize innocent people, shame them, and fuel hatred and animosity. Stephens, however, was positioning himself not only as a defender of other people's liberty but also as a victim. Ignoring his own power and privilege, he convinced himself that he was punching up at the forces of intolerance, when in fact he was punching down on a professor. As Karpf later wrote, "He really needs to learn not to abuse his status to threaten random Twitter users."

---

* It's also reasonable to point out that, as a woman who writes for a living, I had to get a thicker skin than Stephens apparently has, and early on. And I'm white. My friends who are women of color routinely get mobbed with harassing and truly demeaning tweets and comments. So it's all relative, but some people learn about needing thick skin early on.

What's more, Stephens misunderstood the dynamics of the platforms, including the exponential magic of online transmission. When Karpf received Stephens's email, he promptly tweeted about it. As he described in his own op-ed:

Something clicked, and the story went immediately viral. The original joke had zero retweets and nine likes. It now has 4,700 retweets and 31,200 likes. I have spent the past two days in the center of the viral media controversy, instead of observing with interest from the sidelines.

Stephens had equipped the peashooter with his own media battleship. He had tried to shame the professor, and the shame instead came raining down on him. Karpf would go on to teach the encounter in his media classes, he wrote, as a case study of the so-called Streisand Effect:* when authority figures attempt to repress online content but instead their actions draw massive attention to it. This happens with predictable frequency. Those on top protect their own interests, and shame their antagonists, under the guise of defending the greater good.

In July 2020, as protests against police abuses crested around the world and the novel coronavirus swept the globe, a group of 151 authors, artists, and intellectuals put together what they saw as a written defense of free speech. They published it in *Harper's Magazine,* the 170-year-old standard of liberalism. "The democratic inclusion we want can be achieved only if we speak out against the intolerant climate that has set in on all sides," they wrote. They

---

*The singer Barbra Streisand gave birth to this effect, unwittingly, when she sued a photographer in 2003 for distributing aerial photos of her mansion in Malibu, California. When she filed the suit, the online photo had been accessed six times, including twice by Streisand's lawyers. Her suit turned it into a digital sensation.

cited "a vogue for public shaming and ostracism, and the tendency to dissolve complex policy issues in a blinding moral certainty." Editors, they lamented, were fired for running controversial pieces. Academics were investigated for quoting certain works of literature in class. This who's who of arts and letters was defending unencumbered speech, even if what's being said is painful or untrue. Those issues, they argued, should be litigated in the free flow of public debate, not by prohibition, punishment, or decree.

Like Bret Stephens, they made some good points. But like him, they ignored both the power dynamic at play and the direction of their punching. These were some of the most privileged players in the industries of words—journalism, books, theater, and television. Like Stephens, they had enviable platforms. And like him they claimed they were launching their campaign in defense of the broader public.

Their own interests, though, were front and center. They were thought leaders who could publish broadly and promote their brands on TV shows, podcasts, and radio interviews. The voices rising against them, exposing their foibles or prejudices, were becoming a huge inconvenience. They had to be dealt with.

Take J. K. Rowling, one of the signers. A year earlier she had gotten into an ugly row over gender, specifically her quibbles about accepting trans women as women. These are indeed issues people need to talk about. Yet this one, unfortunately, played out on Twitter, and a disproportionate share of humanity's attention was focused on the theories of one woman about a subject that had nothing to do with the source of her fame, Harry Potter. A blizzard of angry and shaming tweets came her way (many of them, doubtless, from people posturing for their friends and followers).

I hated the whole drama. Wouldn't the world be a happier place, I thought, if we didn't have to know what J. K. Rowling thinks about trans women? But Rowling had unveiled her opinion in this digital public square. And now she felt persecuted, victimized. She surely welcomed the chance to sign the Harper's Letter. Get those furious and judgmental people out of my face (and my Twitter feed)!

Her critics looked at it from a different perspective, however: Rowling and her fellow highfliers were shaming them. The letter accused the indignant masses of not just intolerance but shallow thinking, and dividing a complex world into simple dichotomies of good and bad. It accused them of bullying and creating prime conditions for the rise of dangerous demagogues. It was hardly a flattering assessment. In fact, the literary establishment was punching down, and hard.

From the victims' perspective, Rowling had built one of the most massive literary franchises in the history of the planet. Her Harry Potter books and movies and paraphernalia had turned her into that rarest of combinations, a billionaire author. She had what every writer hopes for, an audience ravenous for her words. So when she decided to feature her discomforts surrounding gender on an open forum, were transgender people and their supporters supposed to accept her judgment quietly? Why wouldn't they respond?

The authors attempted, in vain, to position the Harper's Letter as a full-throated defense of the disenfranchised. They argued that "the restriction of debate . . . invariably hurts those who lack power and makes everyone less capable of democratic participation."

But despite this rhetorical flourish, the letter took a stance against the small fry, not on their behalf. The message, after all, was that too many of the presumed powerless were speaking up with their allegedly reductive and censorious online voices. More than a thousand of them took time to comment on *The New York Times*'s coverage of the issue. One, signed DMP from Pennsylvania, asked:

So let me get this straight:

A bunch of rich folks advocating free speech are now offended that others are using their FREE SPEECH to call them out?

So who's trying to silence who?

The authors' self-interest, camouflaged in much of the letter, shines through toward the end, where they demand shelter from any storms of shame that their words might provoke. "As writers," they explain, "we need a culture that leaves us room for experimentation, risk taking, and even mistakes."

Yes, we should all be free to make mistakes. Alabama's George Wallace made his share of them. As he climbed to power, he was downright cruel. At his inauguration as governor of Alabama in 1963, the same year that Martin Luther King, Jr., delivered his "I Have a Dream" speech, Wallace took the opposite approach:

> In the name of the greatest people that have ever trod this earth, I draw a line in the dust and toss the gauntlet before the feet of tyranny, and I say, segregation now, segregation tomorrow and segregation forever.

Racism was Wallace's métier. It fueled his rise to power, both in Alabama and in his national campaigns for the presidency. In the 1968 presidential election, Wallace won five states in the Deep South, even though the presidency ultimately went to Richard Nixon. (No third-party candidate since has garnered a single state.) Wallace dared to say out loud the vicious things that many of his fellow white citizens were thinking. That was his connection.

During this time, shame didn't seem to be an issue for George

Wallace, at least as far as the public could see. Maybe he believed what he said, that segregationist policies were ordained by God and necessary for the defense and well-being of "his people." Or maybe racism was just useful politically.

In either case, something dramatic happened in the spring of 1972. Wallace was in Maryland, campaigning for the Democratic nomination for president, when a would-be assassin named Arthur Bremer shot him. Bremer had initially planned to kill President Nixon, but he decided Wallace would be a much easier target. Bremer shot Wallace four times at point-blank range but failed to kill him. One of the bullets lodged in the governor's spine, paralyzing him from the waist down.

While Wallace was recuperating in the hospital, he had an unexpected visitor: Shirley Chisholm, the first Black woman ever elected to Congress, and also the first to run in a presidential primary. Chisholm had suspended her campaign after the assassination attempt. And over the objections of her staff, she went to see him.

Focusing on the political calculation, Wallace asked Chisholm how her people would respond to her unusual visit. "I know what they're going to say but I wouldn't want what happened to you to happen to anyone," Chisholm said, according to Wallace's daughter, who adds: "Daddy was overwhelmed by her truth, and her willingness to face the potential negative consequences of her political career because of him—something he had never done for anyone else."

Perhaps Wallace felt a smidgen of shame. Maybe his brush with death led him to rethink his priorities for his remaining time on earth. In any case, he underwent a moral metamorphosis. On a Sunday in 1979, Wallace appeared, unannounced, at the Dexter Avenue King Memorial Baptist Church in Montgomery, Alabama. The church was central to the civil rights movement, and four years earlier had been named a National Historic Landmark for its role in American history.

Except for the attendant who rolled his wheelchair to the front of this sanctuary, Wallace was unaccompanied. "I've learned what suffering means in a way that was impossible," he told the congregation. "I think I can understand something of the pain that black people have come to endure. I know I contributed to that pain and I can only ask for your forgiveness."

Two years later, Wallace ran for governor again, this time on a racial unity platform. He won, receiving 90 percent of the African American vote. Seeing that number, you might suspect that it was political calculation on his part to apologize. But that's not unusual or, for that matter, problematic. When we decide to face our shame, whether drug addiction or marital cheating, we always analyze the costs and benefits. What do I have to gain from this? What might I lose? While it's true that being honest and confronting an issue has an immense and often transformative payoff, it can also hurt. Most people will choose to avoid the pain and the reward, but both fit into the equation.

Regardless of his motivation, Wallace made the right choice. He made himself vulnerable to the judgment of his victims. That meant a lot to them. It was a courageous step, one we could all learn from: *I have done wrong. I'm sorry. I ask for your forgiveness.*

CHAPTER 7

REJECTION AND DENIAL

n the hierarchy of status, the only force that can compete with money is sex. It's tied up with survival and preservation of the species. We feel it deep in our animal bodies and souls. It's often seen as a game, where winners have lovers, handsome, beautiful, or rich. The losers sleep alone.

Virginity, for many, is a curse, celibacy a disgrace. So a sexual rejection, or many such rejections, can quickly become a rejection of self. The stakes are high.

Celibates, like every shamed person, face a choice. They can feel miserable about their solitude and simply suffer in loneliness and self-loathing. Or they can try to accept their condition, which is likely temporary, and open up about it, perhaps talking to others about how to resolve it or at least deal with the unhappiness and frustration. This is hard, because getting past shame involves confronting it. In the best case, it would lead to falling in love, or at the very least participating in the social life that can lead to a match.

Another choice, however, is to turn the entire drama on its head and come up with a reason to be proud of celibacy. In the case of the incels, or involuntary celibates, the rejection they suffer becomes a rallying cry for aggrieved online communities. Often spending much of their waking life on Reddit subgroups, incels feed on common myths and narratives, many of them false. And they defend their shared identity with an arsenal of phony science.

The patron saint for many of them is a murderer named Elliot Rodger.

On a spring day in 2014, Rodger, an intensely unhappy student at Santa Barbara City College, uploaded a despairing video to YouTube. In a seven-minute diatribe spoken from the driver's seat of his black BMW, he described how he felt mistreated by women. "For the last eight years of my life, ever since I hit puberty, I've been forced to endure an existence of loneliness, rejection and unfulfilled desires," he said. "Girls gave their affection and sex and love to other men but never to me. I'm 22 years old, and I'm still a virgin. . . . College is the time when everyone experiences those things such as sex and fun and pleasure. All the girls that I have desired so much, they would have looked down on me, and rejected me, as an inferior man. . . . I've had to rot in loneliness."

So Rodger vowed to walk into the "hottest sorority house" of the University of California, Santa Barbara, and "slaughter every single spoiled stuck-up blonde slut I see inside there." He would prove, he said, that he was the "true alpha male."

The following day, Rodger went on his homicidal spree. He shot and killed two sorority members, stabbed to death three young men, including two of his roommates and a guest, and then killed another man and injured fourteen more as he drove around the small town of Isla Vista firing a gun out the car window. Then he shot himself in the head.

Rodger left behind a 140-page manuscript, "My Twisted World," detailing his downward spiral, from childhood in England to adolescence in Los Angeles, where his father worked in the movie industry. As he grew, he developed a deepening rage toward women, for withholding their love, and at other men, for being born with attributes that appealed to women.

In the entire manuscript, Rodger never once used the term "incel." But with his video, his life story, and above all, his violence, he became an idol for the incel community. Four years later, a Toronto man named Alek Minassian praised Rodger on a Facebook post and declared: "The Incel Rebellion has already begun!" Minutes later he plowed his car onto a crowded sidewalk, killing ten people, most of them female. Nikolas Cruz, accused of the 2018 massacre of seventeen students at Marjory Stoneman Douglas High School in Parkland, Florida, had previously posted tributes to Rodger. Like many others, he referred to him as "the Supreme Gentleman." By late 2019, police attributed at least forty-seven killings in North America to people inspired by the networked circles of incels. The number continues to climb.

The incel movement dates back to the dawn of the public internet, in the 1990s. It started on a single website, now long gone, and later took root on blogs and, especially, Reddit subgroups. It is impossible to imagine groups like this existing anywhere but on the internet: Where else could you find so many other rejected, aggrieved men—the vast majority of them white—willing to spend hours complaining about not getting laid? Angry men bonding over shared hatred is nothing new, but the scale and unity of purpose of the incels is an internet-enabled phenomenon.

What incels share is the shame of being unwanted, unloved, rejected. Everyone, in their view, is on a ladder of desirability, and incels are stuck on the lowest rung. Elliot Rodger, in his memoir, recalls stepping out one evening in Isla Vista in his fruitless hunt for love:

> On one of those nights, I crossed paths with a boy who was walking with two pretty girls. I got so envious that I cursed at them, and then I followed them for a few minutes. They just laughed at me, and one of the girls kissed the boy on the lips. I'm assuming she was his girlfriend. That was one of the worst experiences of torture from girls that I've had

to endure, and it will be a scar in my memory forever, to remind me that girls think I'm unworthy compared to other boys. I ran home with tears pouring down my cheeks, hoping that my horrible housemates wouldn't be there to witness my shame.

The incel response to this shame is to amplify and celebrate it—a denial of sorts. Their mutual shame brings them together. And their openness about it puts them all in the same boat, which provides a measure of comfort. In this sense, their Reddit forums are like rehab programs, or Alcoholics Anonymous meetings, where people unburden themselves of shameful secrets. But there are crucial differences. While patients in rehab group sessions are attempting to leave their problems behind, incels glorify their wretched state. And unlike most rehab groups, in which members sit together in a single room or on a solitary Zoom session, incels meet and evangelize on global shame networks. That's where their hopes and dreams devolve into darkness.

"It's like a game of one-upmanship," says Bradley Hinds, a California-based journalist who has followed the online communities. "One person says his life is awful, that he's in the basement and hasn't showered in two weeks, and someone else will say that he's filthy, too, and then add, 'The last time I talked to a girl, she spit in my face.'"

The incel forums are incubators of despair, which generates sporadic violence, both murders and suicides. And their common bond has a significant appeal to a sizable constituency. After all, loads of people find the dating game difficult. The incel groups offer fellowship and a sense of power, along with a framework to explain why the world seems to be so monstrously unfair to them.

These groups represent a different variety of shame engine. They draw in people who suffer from shame and enable them to shift from defensive crouch to attack mode. Only a handful of men turn the rampant misogyny and hatred into murderous violence; the vast majority wage their battles with words. Most sit by themselves, says Hinds, spending nearly every waking hour in the "manosphere," a decentralized complex of gaming platforms, websites, and chat rooms. With their posts, they eviscerate the apparently content and sexually fulfilled people, society's winners. They dehumanize women, often referring to them as "femoids." Indeed, their grievance-fed ideology is bursting with male supremacy and frequently drifts into white supremacy.

Like many shame engines, from the diet industry to pharmaceuticals, the incel community builds its arguments upon a foundation of pseudoscience, attempting to validate it with scraps of biological determinism and evolutionary anthropology. Many of these ideas are accompanied by statistics, giving them the sheen of science. The 80/20 divide, for example, postulates that 80 percent of women focus on the most desirable quintile of males. Most women, the thinking goes, can have sex whenever the urge strikes them. This gives them immense and arbitrary power over the males, especially over those who didn't win the genetic lottery—who lack the height, body type, jawline, and skin color (white) that the women supposedly demand.

They see the jockeying for sexual partners as fundamentally unfair. And they lard their worldview with metrics. This, again, is common to other shame engines. The incels apply metrics to mating, ranking people on a scale. The lucky minority of men, the top percent or two, are matched with high-ranking women, "10s" in the incels' misogynistic parlance. (The male elites are called "Chads," the most desirable women, "Stacys." These privileged few receive nothing but loathing in the incel universe.) The less successful men, much like students destined for second-tier universities, scrounge for less desirable sexual pickings, while an even lower class—abject losers in the genetic lottery—is condemned to a loveless life of celibacy.

Their numbers have little relation to reality. For example, the incels' minority is not so little, or so lonely. The number of celibates in the United States is high, and rising. According to a 2018 *Washington Post* survey, 28 percent of men and 18 percent of women between the ages of eighteen and thirty had not had sexual relations in the previous year. Both rates had more than doubled since 2008. And these statistics no doubt rose during the pandemic. Fewer young people, for one reason or another, are having sex. However, only a fraction of them choose to anchor their identity to their involuntary celibacy and embrace despair.

This hopelessness, oddly, can serve as a balm. If you're convinced that your case is futile, that because of your genes no woman will ever love or accept you, then you can give up on all the self-help, the trips to the gym and the dermatologists, the diets. Forget all that! Despite what you hear, success is not a choice. Accepting this bleak destiny is known as blackpilling. If you put religious faith to one side and replace it with despair, blackpilling is the incel equivalent of the monk's vows of chastity. It is the creed of their order.

Blackpilling is reflected starkly in words bouncing back and forth in their nook of the manosphere. A linguistic analysis of forty-nine thousand postings on incel websites between 2017 and 2019 showed dangerously high levels of "toxicity," much of it marked by anger, fear, and sadness. Researchers compared the language used and sentiments expressed by incels to a random selection of communications in other chat rooms and discovered that incel postings were about three times more likely to feature "toxic, highly toxic, insulting, profane or sexually explicit" content—and, not surprisingly, to be severely lacking in joy.

To sustain and defend its lonely bastion, the community looks to high priests. These are thought leaders whose words bolster their grievances. One shining star in their universe is Jordan Peterson. The Canadian psychologist commands a massive following for his speeches, books, and YouTube videos, by advocating, with an academic air, against political correctness and in defense of the primacy of men. He argues that order is masculine and chaos feminine, and that this has held true since the dawn of our species. This helps explain why men have run the world, and why they should.

Peterson is by no means an incel. But like them, he believes that mating occurs within a ranked marketplace governed by supply and demand. He claims that women are hypergamous, which means that they tend to mate with men of an equal or higher status. "Mate choice is a difficult problem," he argues in a 2018 podcast. "Here's how women solve it. Throw men in a ring. Let them compete at whatever they're competing at. Assume that the man who wins is the best. Marry him." The probability that these winners will have "additional mating opportunities is exceptionally high."

Basically, in incel-speak, the Chads get all the Stacys. Both of these lucky elites wield an abundance of so-called erotic capital, and they enjoy limitless opportunities for fabulous sex with the most enviable partners. This leaves those at the bottom of the hierarchy, the incels, alone with their videogames and online groups. This painful imbalance is fueled by today's information technology. It allows the winners, men and women alike, to shop on dating sites, size up prospects on search engines and social networks, and announce their triumphs, accompanied by photos on Facebook or Instagram.

The dominance of this sexual elite creates unhealthy outcomes and shames those whose erotic capital is low, Peterson says. But he has a solution, which he calls "enforced monogamy." Each alpha male, in this vision, would have to stop sleeping around, quit monopolizing the prime female inventory, and settle for a single woman. This in theory would free up more women for the less attractive males, perhaps including the incels.

Naturally, this idea stirs a wisp of hope for some. But here Peterson cautions that the incels may be getting ahead of themselves. Following his discussion of enforced monogamy in a 2018 *New York Times* article, he responded to subsequent criticism: "The implication was that I wanted to take nubile young women, at the point of the gun, and deliver them under state enforcement to useless men." What he meant instead was that social expectations would uphold monogamy. In other words, philandering Chads would be shamed.

This line of thinking—regulation of the sexual marketplace—leads to all sorts of incel fantasies, such as redistribution of women. Again, contrarian academics, such as Robin Hanson, an economist at George Mason University, throw the incels a line: sex as a welfare benefit. "One might plausibly argue that those with much less access to sex suffer to a similar degree as those with low income," he blogged, "and might similarly hope to gain from organizing around this identity, to lobby for redistribution along this axis and to at least implicitly threaten violence if their demands are not met."

After many horrified Twitter users complained that this sounded like the commodification of the female body, Hanson backtracked—while keeping women firmly in the marketplace. Perhaps the redistribution could be effectuated in cash, he wrote, which could then be used to hire prostitutes.

If you're wondering how things got this crazy, I share your sentiment. But shame is an immensely powerful force, and for people stuck in the stage of denial, where they continuously experience cognitive dissonance, almost anything that sounds good and soothes grievances gets a hearing. For a community like the incels, organized around shared sexual shame and victimhood, such theories are like catnip. They seem to offer a solution to the scourge of celibacy while taking the blame out of it. And if feminists and their politically correct allies complain about it, decrying an evenhanded distribution of sexual opportunity on the grounds that it turns women into property, well, they're just defending the rigged status quo. Among incels, it's a given that women's bodies are and always have been vehicles of desire and fulfillment, and that through the centuries these temptresses have mastered the art of exploiting men's unquenching need for them.

Following this mad line of thought, commanding men who abuse women—bullies like the notorious Hollywood producer Harvey Weinstein—are simply victims of the beautiful women who lure them into such violence. And women, many of whom couldn't even vote or open their own bank accounts until the twentieth century, emerge somehow as the privileged ones in the gender equation.

Movements built upon falsehoods and denial tend to be fragile. The members need one another. Incels are cosseted and sustained by the manosphere, with its nonthreatening games and virtual friendships. But no matter how long and faithfully they remain there, they cannot help but know that there's a big and bustling world outside, where people carry on along traditional pathways, pursuing relationships and families. And most of those people consider incel ideology ludicrous, if they've even heard of it. What's more, many of them don't seem to be stunted in spite of weak chins, pimples, weight problems, body odor, unemployment, or a host of other shortcomings that incels view as disqualifying them from ordinary life. This cannot be kept secret from them. Incels are not hermetically sealed off from the rest of the world.

They know that any day, members of their cohort might desert. Some, clearly, are itching to. Growing numbers of them are undergoing extreme plastic surgery in hopes of becoming more attractive to women—and looking more like "Chads." These people are entertaining grave doubts about their submission to hopelessness, their blackpilling. They want out.

Occasionally, a member of the incel community happens upon an alternative way of seeing things. He might meet a nice girl after biology class, says Bradley Hinds, and strike up a conversation. The next thing his fellow incels know, he goes poof, disappearing from the chat room, and maybe from the entire manosphere. (All too often, tragically, the disappearances are suicides.)

For the remaining incels, each desertion suggests the possibility of a reality that might work better than the bleak existence they've settled into—this nonstop grievance-filled shamefest, all of it occurring on a screen. Maybe the entire incel experience is nothing but a misery-loves-company detour in life. Could it be possible that their loneliness is not handed down by fate—bad luck in the genetic lottery—but instead a choice?

This goes against the founding thesis of the community. There's a reason they call their celibacy "involuntary." However, the thought has to occur to them that it just might be in their power to brighten their dark days with love, and to escape inceldom.

This is the inherent instability within belief groups and cults, from Scientology to ISIS. Deserters and people at the edges pose a steady threat. For true believers, the ones more invested in the cult, the tenuous fabric of their worldview, with its cognitive dissonance and its fraying at the seams, can push them away from doubt and toward a harder line, and orthodoxy. The most ardent manage to shut their eyes and plug their ears to widely accepted truths as they construct their own catechism, a point-by-point rebuttal of the Chads' and Stacys' view of things.

As a result, incels' deep shame, and their contempt for mainstream mores and political correctness, can bring them into harmony with all sorts of unsavory allies. Some find common cause with white supremacists.* One ideology that appeals to both groups is a proposal known as replacement theory. The idea is that women in the developed world now have far too much latitude to pursue careers and other interests. They are able to delay child-bearing, or even avoid it altogether. This dampens the growth of the white population and undermines the demographic foothold of white power. The fear is that people who appear to keep their women in line—think Muslims and Mexicans—will overwhelm the white world with billions of darker babies. This is a close cousin of the paternalistic misogyny voiced by Jordan Peterson. And its solution is similar, if more racial: Find ways to force white women to bear more offspring. This might lead them to sexual partners they would not otherwise choose—perhaps expanding available inventory to incels.

I spent some time in Japan while working on this book.† With my focus on shame, I paid special attention to a group of teens and young adults called *hikikomori*. Numbering in the hundreds of thousands, these young people have retreated from Japanese society, taking refuge in their bedrooms in their parents' homes. While the percentage of women has been rising as researchers train their sights on locked-in housewives, historically, the majority of hikiko-mori have been men.

Most hikikomori do not work or study. They have few friends, and by definition have spent at least six months in isolation.

*For more on this intersection, see Talia Lavin's book, *Culture Warlords*.

†I learned a lot. For example, you compliment a chef by savoring his or her rice. It is the purest expression of their mastery. And to drown rice in soy sauce is a desecration and an insult to the chef.

Sekiguchi Hiroshi, a psychiatrist who has studied the hikikomori, says that they "feel a deep sense of shame that they cannot work at a job like ordinary people. They think of themselves as worthless and unqualified for happiness." They're remorseful, he adds, for "having betrayed their parents' expectations."

The extreme measures that some take to disappear are heartbreaking. Sekiguchi writes that many keep their curtains and shutters closed at all times, and mute the sound when they watch TV or use the computer. They walk softly, creeping into the kitchen to raid the refrigerator at night while other family members sleep. Some forgo air conditioners and heating, sweltering in summer, freezing in winter, not only to avoid announcing their presence by making noise but also "because they do not feel they deserve to use these appliances."

Like incels, the hikikomori feel unworthy so they withdraw. They have no one to tell them that their lives hold meaning. Every day that no one knocks on their door and no one calls, the entire world, it might seem, is affirming their harsh self-judgment. No one, with the exception of their worried family members, wants to be with them.

In rare cases, this has driven individual hikikomori, like incels, to murderous violence. In June 2020, a twenty-three-year-old recluse living near Kobe admitted to killing three family members with a crossbow and injuring a fourth.

But the vast majority of them simmer in their loneliness. This they share with too many others. Loneliness is a growing epidemic in the industrialized world, and the coronavirus exacerbated it, leading to a spike in suicides and overdoses. This is typical of shame in many of its manifestations, and it's a natural response. Whether their shame is stoked by obesity, poverty, addiction, or sexual inadequacy, people who feel vulnerable to judgment shield themselves from others. This, like many forms of shame, creates a self-reinforcing cycle. The shame leads to loneliness, and the lonely are all too likely to punish themselves for having few friends. So they feel even worse—and more removed from people who might tell them that they're loved.

Naturally, the sad plight of the hikikomori creates markets for shame industries. Many of them now service the lock-ins. The greatest financial opportunities come not from selling directly to the hikikomori but instead to their parents, many of whom, desperate for a solution, are themselves victims of the deepest shame. In a culture that esteems hard work and professional success, their children have locked themselves away and surrendered. A hikikomori hidden in his bedroom for ten years can stigmatize an entire family. When visitors come, parents keep their ears pricked (a good number of them hoping, no doubt, that the recluse behind the closed door doesn't announce his presence by turning on the TV). In some cases, the parents' shame is so great that they, too, become recluses.

Expensive consultants now offer to solve the problem for anxious parents. They're called *hikidashiya,* or "those who pull people out." They charge tens of thousands of dollars to draw recluses from their rooms and integrate them into the working world. Some successfully coax the hikikomori from their lairs and lead them outside. Others break through the door and drag them out, pushing them into a van and rushing them away.

A complaint to Tokyo police in 2020 charged that one hikidashiya had forcibly removed a young man from his room, plunked him into a psychiatric hospital for fifty days, and from there transferred him to a locked-down dormitory. For this, the parents had paid $65,000. Reminiscent of the legions of addiction rehab scams, some hikidashiya take away the hikikomori's money and phones, preventing contact with their families, and force them into work camps.[*]

As I delved into these dark channels of shame and isolation, I couldn't help but worry about my three sons. Sites on the internet offered refuge and community. They promised relief from the exquisitely awkward phases of puberty, with its insecurity, sexual frustration, and occasional rage. My sons were grappling with masculinity, which imposes its own narrow pathways of acceptable behavior. That hadn't been my issue, of course. But I knew that if I'd had access to online worlds when I was a kid, I probably would have burrowed into some kind of emo death cult.

I talked to other parents about the rabbit holes our boys could fall into. They worried, they said, as their kids spouted bits of right-wing extremism at the dinner table, often in an ironic jokey way, or defended hate speech as free speech. The boys were tiptoeing around incel ideas but hadn't taken the plunge.

Then one boy did. He was now a self-described incel. His father told me that his son was spending all his time in his room and was spewing hatred toward his mother and the outside world. In fits of rage, the father told me, his wife had tried to shame her son away from his toxic community. She pointed out how wrongheaded he was, how cruel he had become, and how he was way too privileged to be playing the victim. It was an all-out war in his house, and the father didn't see it ending anytime soon. Desperate, he asked me for advice.

I suspected that their son was looking for a community and an

---

[*]You might notice that this is the only chapter that doesn't point, at least primarily, to a profit motive, at least beyond the plastic surgeons, the hikidashiya, and thought leaders such as Jordan Peterson. People who are essentially removed from society represent less of a commercial opportunity than those who are willing to spend anything to fit in.

identity that promised relief from sexual frustration and exclusion. These behaviors typically spike after periods of transition, such as starting at a new school without friends. They also often pass. But to shame them for this detour risks driving them further into it. What's more, the boy probably saw through the nonsense people were putting forth on the sites but stuck with it for the camaraderie. By studying the men who emerged from hate groups, the sociologist Michael Kimmel provides at least an inkling of the dynamics. Most of them, it turned out, didn't believe in the ideology of the group they'd left. Many never had. They had joined for a sense of brotherhood and belonging.

At those vulnerable moments, perhaps the best we can do for our children is to offer other options, different avenues to explore away from the shame networks. They should know that they can make mistakes and experiment with their identities. The most important thing we can give them is the confidence that when they emerge, they will find love and forgiveness.

PART III

HEALTHY
SHAME

CHAPTER 8

THE COMMON GOOD

G iddy with excitement, a small crowd streamed into a Target store in Fort Lauderdale, Florida, for an act of civil disobedience. It was September 2020, about six months into the COVID-19 pandemic in the United States. In keeping with the store's rules, everyone in the group wore masks. As they formed a circle, shouting and whooping it up, they pulled out their cellphones and began taking videos. Then the protest commenced. Tearing off their face masks, they circulated en masse through the store, yelling, "Take off your masks! We're Americans!"

This exuberant group of rule breakers surrounded masked shoppers and encouraged them to rip off their face gear. Some shoppers edged away, trying to avoid confrontation (and health risks). Others conformed to the shaming, obediently removing their masks. Each one sparked jubilation from the protesters. Another convert to their cause.

Throughout the pandemic, the mask became a locus of shame. The protesters in that Florida Target were performing for their friends and followers on shame networks. And with this performance, they shamed masked shoppers for bending timidly to authority, for being sheep. Others, meanwhile, shamed people for neglecting to wear masks. As Supreme Court Justice Clarence Thomas reflected, "There is some degree of opprobrium if one does not wear it in certain settings."

The conflicting shame streams were each anchored to a core social value. For the Target demonstrators, it was the defense of freedom. Those who complied with the mandates—to stretch the anti-maskers' argument to its hyperbolic extreme—were undermining the self-determination that thousands of American soldiers had fought and died for over centuries, not to mention the vision of our forefathers enshrined in the Constitution.

That argument, naturally, sounded outlandish to people living in hot zones. During the first devastating COVID-19 outbreak, those of us in New York had lain awake night after night as an ambulance shrieked through the darkness. Many had lost friends and relatives to the pandemic, and thousands were risking their lives in hospitals and clinics as they worked frantically to save others. The guiding mission, by strong consensus, was to protect the health of the community, especially the more vulnerable among us. To do this, most of us heeded what the scientists had been telling us with increasing urgency: Face masks shield people from the virus, including exploited frontline workers. Wear one! From the perspective of my neighborhood, wearing a mask was like stopping at a traffic light. It was an inconvenience that reduced the risk that we'd kill one another. Our responsibility to one another outweighed the minor infringement on our freedom that the mask represented. We enforced this rule with shame.

A month or two into the pandemic, my husband ventured out on the street without a mask. He'd forgotten it. He stayed a good distance from others on the sidewalk. But he felt the shaming stares. Someone even said something nasty to him. He came inside angry and visibly stung. Already at work on this book, I was interested to see how the shame affected him. The result was decisive. From that day forward, he made sure to wear his mask. In a community of shared values, from a Pueblo gathering in New

Mexico to New York's Upper West Side, there's no greater power than shame to bring people into line.

But on social networks, shaming mask skeptics can come across as a self-righteous gesture, as virtue signaling. I saw it playing out on my social media feeds. People indignantly posted spring break photos of college students cavorting without masks in Florida bars and on beaches. "We are desperate for an outlet, and indoor finger-pointing is one of the few hobbies still accessible to those sheltering in place," wrote Amanda Hess, a *New York Times* columnist.

Those tut-tuts elicited mocking taunts from the anti-maskers. They didn't share the same norms and seemed impervious to the shaming. They were bolstered in their defiance by the Trump White House and its allies, who politicized the issue, associating mask-wearing with cowardice. They turned it into a xenophobic meme, calling it the "Chinese" virus. A Twitter user writing as @soniapatriot weighed in: "The way the sheep are going crazy about masks is like MASKS are the cure for China virus!! First China sends the virus and then we buy masks made in China. All sheep have a choice. Stay home and stay muzzled." The tweet has since been deleted. In her eyes, their mask-wearing was a physical signal of submission to fear and hypochondria and foreign invaders.

Meanwhile, smaller dramas were taking place all over the country, from sidewalk cafés to softball games. Robert Klitzman, a psychiatry professor at Columbia University, described the awkwardness of being the only person at a party to wear a mask: "Two people strolled over, about two to three feet from me, unmasked and drinking beers. They seemed a bit uneasy, as if guilty about their uncovered faces, and I felt as if they were wondering whether I was somehow therefore judging them, or didn't fully trust them, or was merely being unsociable."

When the virus started claiming lives in Mitchell, South

Dakota, the debate over a mask mandate seemed to tear the town in half. At a contentious meeting, according to *The Washington Post*, opponents of masks argued that a host of pseudoscientific defenses would keep the virus at bay. They ranged from diets of wild-caught sardines and pasture-raised beef liver to raw kombucha. And one woman compared the anti-maskers' lot to that of Jews under Adolf Hitler. "The bare face is the new yellow star of Nazi Germany," she said. This line was picked up the following year by Marjorie Taylor Greene, the QAnon-backing Republican congresswoman from Georgia.

As the virus spread, a combative point of view became, more and more, the refuge of the politically indoctrinated. One of them, it turned out, worked under Dr. Anthony Fauci, who was heading the government's effort to control the pandemic. Bill Crews, a public affairs official at the National Institute of Allergy and Infectious Diseases, was excoriating his own colleagues online. Writing under a pseudonym on the right-wing site RedState, Crews lambasted the people mandating masks and shutdowns. "If there were justice, we'd send [a] few dozen of these fascists to the gallows and gibbet their tarred bodies in chains until they fall apart," he wrote in June of that year. This, of course, was madness. And three months later, when he was exposed and fired, many of his supporters had probably already masked up, however grudgingly.

We wouldn't see such conflict if it concerned carrying umbrellas in the rain or wearing floppy hats as a defense against skin cancer. But masks are different. Unlike umbrellas or hats, they are important for protecting others, for preventing a killer virus from spreading within the community. In that sense, they offer a perfect opportunity for healthy shaming.

In the beginning, masks faced barriers—political and scientific. The politicization of the issue slowed down acceptance of mask-wearing. What's more, in the first months of the pandemic in the United States, the disease was concentrated in big liberal cities, like New York and Seattle, where more people were wearing masks. As thousands died there, it could be argued that the masks weren't doing much good. For that brief time, anti-maskers in rural Republican zip codes, from Oklahoma to North Dakota, could celebrate their facial freedom. It didn't seem like they would pay a price for it.

The halting steps of science also undermined confidence in masks. The early guidance was to avoid them, because they might induce panic. What's more, the short supply of surgical masks was needed for doctors and nurses tending to COVID-19 patients. The specialists, led by Dr. Anthony Fauci, quickly changed their tune. But the early flip-flop fed the political trope that scientists were as clueless as the rest of us.

This wasn't true, of course. And if we step back and look at the progression of mask-wearing during the pandemic, it provides a case study for both the benefits and the limitations of a healthy shame campaign. Wearing a mask was in the interest of society, and it wasn't hard, unlike the punching-down messaging of shame we read about in the first two parts of this book. People didn't have to get a good job to comply, lose a hundred pounds, or kick a drug habit. All they had to do was strap on a mask when mingling with others. (Prisons, where the inmates were often not supplied with masks even if they wanted one, were an exception to this simple choice.) Over the course of the pandemic, it became increasingly clear that transmission occurred via droplets in the air, and the urgent need for mask-wearing grew. The border between the two warring sides began to shift. Now that it was a question of self-preservation, growing numbers of people started to accept a version of truth they'd previously rejected. Even the governors of Texas, Florida, and Georgia, who had resisted protective measures for months, reluctantly issued mask mandates.

The to-mask-or-not-to-mask controversy replicated at light-ning speed the decades-long drama around smoking cigarettes. Throughout most of the twentieth century, smokers felt free to surround themselves with toxic clouds, regarding those who com-plained as worrywarts. Shaming smokers for their secondhand smoke worked only in the small circles where people paid atten-tion to emerging research about the risks. In 1998, when California banned smoking in public places, including bars and restaurants, smokers threatened boycotts and protests, and accused the gov-ernment of infringing on their freedom. Similar hand-wringing followed five years later, when New York City mayor Michael Bloomberg followed suit. Yet by the end of that decade, smoking in bars was not only unlawful in much of the world but deemed inconsiderate, even in former smoker paradises, such as Paris and Rome. It was not just the new laws that had changed the norms but also a clearer understanding of the danger.

The same dynamic began to undermine the anti-maskers. While the acceptance of masks was far from universal—especially grating to urbanites in red states—the progress in only one year was notable. Within months, it became harder for anti-maskers to ignore evidence that disproved their "facts." Increasingly, outside of defiant anti-masking groups, donning a face covering no longer appeared to be signaling virtue, in the same way that stopping at a red light isn't worthy of applause. People were simply being pru-dent, and sane.

One trouble with shame, though, is that it tends to splash around. Some of it spilled onto the victims of the disease. They were the ones, after all, who had let their guard down. And with every breath they were endangering everyone else. In a 2020 Johns Hopkins study, 42 percent of Americans agreed that "people who get COVID-19 have behaved irresponsibly." One result of this judgment was that many victims of COVID-19 were reluctant to seek help: They withdrew or were in denial because they were ashamed. This was counterproductive, of course, and not only for the victims. It also raised the risks for everyone else.

Shaming the afflicted is yet another form of punching down. It's ineffective and unfair. In this case, many poor and working people, whether cashiers at the supermarket or receptionists at an urgent care center, had to put themselves in danger to make a living. When they fell ill, they were victims in the truest sense. Shaming them for their misfortune exonerated people in power and shifted the blame to essential workers.

While COVID-shaming is toxic, I'd argue that the shame my husband endured for walking barefaced was justified and healthy. Mask-wearing is a choice. Shaming someone for not wearing one is viable as a tactic, even necessary. A virus, it goes without saying, is a hazard that society has a right to police. In this sense, the pandemic created a new norm, and a new form of shame evolved to enforce it.

To be sure, its success was far from universal. In our diverse and polarized society, that's nearly impossible. However, this new form of healthy shame notched a victory of sorts. It didn't necessarily feel good—just ask my husband. But it was legitimate, and it worked.

In the history of pandemics, smallpox was much more deadly than COVID-19. It was particularly brutal in the eighteenth century, killing an average of four hundred thousand Europeans annually. However, one sector of society seemed to be spared the ravages. In villages and households where the virus wiped out entire families, milkmaids, for some reason, escaped unharmed.

Toward the end of that century, a British doctor named Edward Jenner came up with a theory to explain this resistance. It was well known that people who survived one bout of smallpox did not contract it a second time. In previous decades, a number of people had sought protection by scratching their skin and infecting themselves with what they hoped would be minor cases of smallpox. Benjamin Franklin, who lost a four-year-old son to the disease in 1736, regretted for the rest of his life that he hadn't preemptively infected the boy. These inoculations, though, were risky, resulting in death about 2 percent of the time. Perhaps, Jenner thought, the itchy disease the milkmaids contracted from cattle—cowpox—could provide similar protection without the risk.

On a spring day in 1796, Jenner conducted an experiment. Cowpox, he was told, had erupted on the hands and forearms of a local milkmaid named Sarah Nelmes. He would harvest pus from her pox and use it to inoculate a test subject. Then he'd see if that human guinea pig was immune to smallpox.

Jenner selected an eight-year-old boy, James Phipps, the son of his gardener, to receive the first inoculation. In the following days, the boy suffered mild symptoms, apparently from cowpox. Jenner then had to verify that his therapy had worked. So he gave the boy what would be a deadly dose of smallpox. The boy survived. Just to make sure, Jenner went on to infect him twenty more times with smallpox pus. The boy's defenses held it off. It was this successful experiment that gave birth to the first vaccine. (The name derives from *vacca,* the Latin word for cow.)

Jenner's vaccine is one of science's triumphs. It eliminated mankind's deadliest disease. And this success established the pathway for further breakthroughs, against polio, diphtheria, whooping cough, measles, and many other scourges. With vaccines, we humans figured out how to hack our own immune systems to defend ourselves.

However, our advances are guided by moral choices, some of them valuing certain lives over others. This feeds skepticism around vaccines, and often resistance. A good starting point is the dynamic between Edward Jenner and eight-year-old James Phipps. Jenner's goal, as a doctor and scientist, was to find a cure. In his view, many lives saved were worth far more than one life risked, especially that of a lowborn boy. On the social scale of eighteenth-century Britain, Jenner occupied a master's caste. He had servants, including his landless gardener and the gardener's son. This gave him the authority, in the name of science, to put the child's life at risk.

It was in the interest of society, as enunciated by a person in a position of power and knowledge, that permitted Jenner to steamroll the rights of an individual, especially a poor one.

It would be outlandish, of course, to compare the helpless James Phipps to someone in modern-day Los Angeles or Brooklyn who resists vaccination against smallpox or COVID-19. Phipps received lethal doses of a deadly disease with no guarantee that Jenner's hunch would pay off, while today's vaccines undergo intensive rounds of testing, for both safety and effectiveness, before gaining approval from the Food and Drug Administration.

Still, the drama around vaccines boils down as always to the reasoning of the scientific elite, who invoke the greater good. In the process, members of this order often shame the recalcitrant for not knowing better. Proponents can assert that the various arguments against vaccines, including a debunked and retracted 1998 paper linking them to childhood autism, are larded with fake science and conspiracy theories. This is true. They can also cite statistics showing the danger from vaccines is minuscule, and the perils of the unvaccinated contracting these diseases are far greater.

Still, a good number of people distrust vaccines. This turned into a divisive issue during the 2010s as communities, from the posh Los Angeles suburb of Santa Monica to the Hasidic neighborhoods of Brooklyn, rebelled against mandatory childhood vaccines. When measles broke out in their schools, politicians, health officials, and news anchors were quick to shame them. This growing skepticism was deeply concerning as COVID-19 spread around the world. The virus was bound to thrive and mutate within unvaccinated populations.

If we look at the crisis as a matter of the community's health and survival, the COVID vaccine seemed like a textbook opportunity to deploy healthy shame. Getting vaccinated kept people from dying and was good for society. Statistics showed that vaccines worked, and that the risks were tiny. What's more, passing up a vaccine was a form of freeloading, leaving the work of building herd immunity to others. Those who didn't take the trouble to get vaccinated, it could be argued, were lazy, selfish, and ignorant. The justification for shaming could hardly be clearer.

But this is one case in which societal shaming turns out to be counterproductive. Shame coming from political leaders or health officials can send people running in the opposite direction. Surveys show that many African Americans, for example, are skeptical of vaccines. Many of them know all too well about the horrors visited upon their community by medical authorities. The infamous Tuskegee experiment, launched in 1932, conducted human trials on Black males, leaving hundreds untreated for syphilis even though they were diagnosed. In 1950, an African American woman named Henrietta Lacks went to the hospital with an advanced case of cervical cancer. Without her knowledge or consent, doctors harvested her cancer cells, which reproduced at an exceptional rate. Lacks died, but her cells went on to become a standard line for oncology research to this day. They were even used in the hunt for COVID-19 vaccines. These stories, along with the systemic medical racism experienced daily by people of color, feed a natural reluctance to get vaccinated.

Hasidic Jews in New York also distrust authorities—nearly all of them outsiders to their community. Shame campaigns from on high only confirm the common suspicion among the Hasidim that the political and economic elite hold them in contempt. In the spring of 2020, during the early days of the pandemic, New York City officials, including Mayor Bill de Blasio, shamed the Hasidic communities in Brooklyn for holding a large and mask-free wedding. The city imposed the strictest lockdown on the zip codes of ultra-Orthodox communities. This shaming fueled powerful resistance. In multiple protests, angry Hasidic men burned their masks.

Part of the problem comes from science itself. Thanks to its rigor, it represents humanity's best bet for figuring things out, whether it's evidence for global warming or effective therapies for shingles. But the communication of science has been botched by politicians, universities, the media, and scientists themselves. It has been enshrined as an unassailable marvel of progress, a producer of truth. But in the culture wars, its defenders often come across as arrogant. They dismiss doubters and contrarians as ignorant or portray them as credulous followers of idiotic conspiracy theories.

This is shaming, and people pick up on it. For many, science now represents only the values of the elite, who also benefit from turbocharged tech, pharma, and finance stocks. From the perspective of the aggrieved lower orders, the elite not only lay claim to the lion's share of wealth but also see themselves as arbiters of truth. "There's an anti-authority feeling in the world," said Dr. Anthony Fauci at the height of the COVID-19 pandemic. "Science has an air of authority to it. So people who want to push back on authority tend to, as a sidebar, push back on science."

Not all vaccine skeptics are ignorant, by any stretch of the imagination. An alarming number of health workers, for example, resisted taking the COVID vaccine in 2021, even after tending for months to victims suffering in their emergency wards on any given day. For example, a group of 117 employees sued Houston Methodist Hospital in May 2021 for mandating staff-wide vaccines. The plaintiffs argued that the vaccines were an experimental therapy. This was hardly a knee-jerk rejection of science. According to Kristen Choi, a registered nurse and an assistant professor at the UCLA School of Nursing, some of her colleagues objected to the frantic pace of the vaccine development, suspecting that corners were cut. Others had witnessed what they viewed as shoddy experiments within their own institutions. That fed their skepticism. "Nurses are not declining because they don't understand research," Choi tweeted. "They're often declining because they DO understand research."

For many, including the nurses Choi knows, the vaccine push must come from people they trust, not distant authorities. Whether it's African Americans in Detroit, Hasidic Jews in New York, or pandemic deniers at a California hot yoga studio, doubters are far more likely to heed those who can attest to their love and support for them—their families, friends, neighbors, congregations.*

In an evangelical church in Orlando, Florida, for example, in early 2021, a reverend named Gabriel Salguero urged his largely Spanish-speaking congregation to get vaccinated. "In getting yourself vaccinated, you are helping your neighbor," he preached. "God wants you to be whole so you can care for your community. So think of vaccines as part of God's plan." Katie Jackson, pastor at Bethany United Church of Christ in Ephrata, Pennsylvania, told her worshippers that God had given them "the technology to protect ourselves." We should make use of it, she said, "not only because of our best interest, but in the interest of others."

That may not sound like shame. But in framing vaccinations as a responsibility to the community, and to God, these ministers were delivering a mild dose of shame. The implication, after all, was

---

*Months into the vaccination campaign, when the safety issue became clearer and the more contagious Delta variant drove up hospitalizations, government officials and corporate leaders grew more comfortable mandating vaccination.

that those who refused to get vaccinated were turning their back on their fellow congregants and saying no to God's plan.

Even in this age of shame networks and punching down, healthy shame can still work its magic. But it must come through doors and windows that are open, not those that are shuttered. Friends and allies know where those openings are, and how to get the message across most effectively. Far better than Bill Gates or Dr. Fauci, they can deliver the kind of gentle shame that signals love. That alone can give us a powerful push in the right direction.

CHAPTER 9

PUNCHING UP

For years, Nigerians had been victimized by corrupt police. One especially noxious branch, the Special Anti-Robbery Squad, or SARS, was notorious for extortion and brutality. Their roadblocks functioned as nets, and the people they ensnared faced no end of trouble. Some were sent to jail on trumped-up charges, where according to Amnesty International they were subjected to degrading treatment and torture. SARS officials helped themselves to people's phones, laptops, jewelry, and even fancy cars. Far worse, they also raped their victims and carried out extrajudicial killings.

In short, they were a plague on society. And this sordid status quo was supported by government officials, who no doubt claimed a share of the proceeds. Nigerians were sick of it, and in 2017, a shaming campaign on social media spread across the country. They shamed the police and the government that held them in place, calling them murderers, thieves, and thugs. This campaign extended from the coastal expanse of Lagos to the desert city of Kano in the north. Yet while the hashtag #EndSARS caught on quickly, the movement didn't explode onto the streets until three years later. In October 2020, following new reports of SARS torture and killings, the protests grew into a national force, one that quickly expanded in scope from policing to broader issues of social justice. Thanks to social media, it was soon reverberating around the world.

The #EndSARS movement, like many others, took on power with shame. The drumbeat of its messaging, whether on billboards, body paint, or tweets, was that these police were acting like animals. It stigmatized the entire force. This approach makes sense, because the world's downtrodden have few other options. They can strike, which strangles them economically. They can rise up in violence, which invites retaliation and death. Or they can shame. In their protests, the message follows a consistent line: The oppressors are behaving abominably. They're shirking their duties and betraying the values they espouse. The hope is that shame will push them to clean up their behavior.

Protests, in this sense, serve the same function as the shaming clowns of the Pueblo Indians. In those ceremonies, as we saw, the clowns focused on members of the community who were not hewing to social standards, whether cheating on their spouses or bootlegging. The purpose of the clowns' shaming was to bring them back into the fold.

The #EndSARS protests functioned in a similar way, but with an important difference: It was leaders of the community who were straying from shared values. By shaming their persecutors, the underdogs attempted to bring these miscreants back into line, or to replace them.

Shame, as we've seen, is a toxin. Sometimes it nudges people toward common values, like donning a mask during a pandemic. But more often, it makes its targets feel wounded, guilty, and, sometimes, worthless. Amid this kind of punitive shaming, the only happy stories involve people like Blossom Rogers and David Clohessy, who succeed in freeing themselves, as much as they can, from shame, and finding a measure of peace.

But the shaming of the powerful—punching up—finally puts

this toxin to constructive use.* Think of righteous protest movements, from civil rights in America to anti-apartheid in South Africa. In these campaigns, those exploited or deprived of their rights effectively shamed the people and institutions holding them down. The abolitionist leader Frederick Douglass, an escaped slave, had a singular mission: "to shame [America] out of her adhesion to a system so abhorrent to Christianity and to her republican institutions."

The hope is that punching up will force the people calling the shots—police chiefs, governors, CEOs—to reexamine their behavior. They'll find themselves embarrassed to answer their children's questions at the dinner table and to face shaking heads and wagging fingers at church. Their reputations will take a beating. They'll feel like bad people. They'll lose political support or paying customers and will change course.

This succeeds, I should note, only when the shamers and the shamed accept the same norms and agree on relevant facts. So shame delivers results in cases where bedrock values are agreed upon and the indiscretion is clear and documented, impossible to deny.

In starting out, a punching-up campaign has to mark these contrasts, with Good and Bad as clearly scripted as in an old cowboy movie. The oppressed must establish themselves as not only righteous but also virtuous, defenders of common values. If it turns out that they're not living by the standards they invoke, or if they are seen to be arguing only on their own behalf, and not for a larger group of worthy individuals, their campaign peters out.

Beyond protesting the abuses of the powerful, punching-up campaigns also provoke those same abuses, ideally for all to see.

---

*For many more examples on this more positive use of shame, see Jennifer Jacquet's book *Is Shame Necessary?*

Demonstrators get beaten, trampled, attacked by police dogs, tear-gassed, fire-hosed. Some of them get killed. These victims often figure prominently into the movements. And martyrs rise to an exalted role. In Nigeria's #EndSARS uprising, fifty-six people died in the first two weeks of protest, some at the hands of security forces, others felled by government-backed gangs.

One of the victims was twenty-eight-year-old Anthony Unuode. He had graduated with an education degree from Nasarawa State University, close to the capital, Abuja. But like most graduates of his generation, he couldn't find a job in his field. The system, it seemed, fell short for people like him—strivers without money or connections. So he set out on his own, running three online betting shops while working as a real estate agent. His father had died years earlier, leaving him as the breadwinner of his family. Unuode had recently filled out papers to enlist in the army. His goal, his friends later said, was to fight the militant Islamist group Boko Haram, which had been carrying out a brutal insurgency in Nigeria's north.

When protesters took to the streets, Unuode joined them. One night, pro-government thugs attacked an #EndSARS rally at an intersection in Abuja. Unuode, witnesses later remembered, shielded fellow protesters with his body, escaping with only a minor injury to his arm.

Four days later, as he and his comrades marched along an expressway in Abuja, pro-government goons fell upon them with machetes, daggers, and wooden sticks. Unuode suffered deep machete wounds to his cranium. He took off his shirt and wrapped it around his head to stanch the bleeding. Then he ran to the home of his friend Muazu Suleiman, who put him in his car and drove him to the national hospital. But according to Suleiman, the caregivers there had no gloves or bandages, and very little medicine. Suleiman hurried out and bought them. When he got back, the electricity in the hospital had gone out. The doctors used cellphone lights as they tried, in vain, to save Unuode's life.

Several days later, protesters held a candlelight vigil to honor Anthony Unuode—and shame the government. His story, as recalled by his brother and friends, drew the sharpest possible moral contrast between good and evil. Unuode was brave, dedicated to his family and country, and hardworking. The government, by contrast, oversaw an economy that didn't give people like him a chance. It presided over a brutal police force and hired armed henchmen to batter its citizens. The government didn't even provide basic medical supplies or electricity for the hospitals that Unuode and the vast majority of the two hundred million Nigerians depended on for their lives.

This was the punching-up message at the vigil that night in Abuja. The forces that ruled Nigeria had killed this innocent man, among many others. In doing so, they had betrayed society's values, as laid out in the 1999 constitution. Written and enacted after the return to democracy from military rule, it promoted "the good government and welfare of all persons in our country, on the principles of freedom, equality and justice, and for the purpose of consolidating the unity of our people." The president, Muhammadu Buhari, expressed his commitment to these principles in a 2019 tweet, which he "pinned" to the top of his Twitter account: "We have no other motive than to serve Nigeria with our hearts and might, and build a nation which we and generations to come can be proud of."

These lofty aspirations opened Buhari to shaming, and the protests and media coverage forced him to defend himself. The usual response in these scenarios is to present an alternative narrative, accusing the protesters themselves of the abuses and dismissing their denunciations as "fake news." But Buhari had to tread carefully, because phone videos on social media showed government forces shooting into apparently peaceful crowds.

Consequently, the president expressed regret for the killings of protesters and conceded that a few policemen had acted badly. But he charged groups of demonstrators with fomenting anarchy. This way he muddied the lines between good and bad, innocent and guilty, and positioned himself as a guardian of democracy. In a crafted statement, Buhari avoided leveling specific accusations—which could conceivably be disproven by videos—by describing the horrors in the passive voice. "Human lives have been lost," he tweeted. "Acts of sexual violence have been reported; two major correctional facilities were attacked and convicts freed; public and private properties completely destroyed or vandalised."

Meanwhile, the leaders of the protest, whether free or in jail, found themselves loathed by large sectors of society. This is common with punching-up shame. It's caused not only by the lies and distortions of the government but also by the discomfort the protesters stir up. Many are viewed as troublemakers even by those who share their goals. Some icons of punching up who are later lionized, like Martin Luther King, Jr., are resented, and often despised, in their own times. They appear selfish, looking to profit from other people's pain. They create traffic jams and shut down commerce. They disrupt.

President Buhari stoked these resentments as they flared up around the #EndSARS protests and battled the movement with both propaganda and muscle. He used messaging to divert the shame, while dispatching riot squads to quell the protesters, killing some, jailing others.

The protesters, meanwhile, appealed for international support. Nigeria, as the most populous country in Africa, has an immense diaspora, especially in North America and Europe, and the nation is well represented in sports and the arts. It didn't take long for word to spread to global celebrities, including Beyoncé, Rihanna, and the German Turkish soccer star Mesut Özil, who tweeted to his twenty-five million followers. The punching-up campaign went viral.

As the protests dissipated in 2021, the #EndSARS movement had notched significant success. Responding to popular pressure, the government disbanded the SARs forces. But the movement broadened its focus to issues of corruption and injustice. While President Buhari survived the protests, his popularity plummeted. More important, he and his colleagues are aware that they are being scrutinized, and that a single incident of abuse can awaken a national shaming campaign in a matter of hours. The punching-up protesters have demonstrated their power.

Mahatma Gandhi, the twentieth century's master of punching up, demonstrated the strategy and discipline required to win the long game. His Salt March in 1930 set the standard. At that time, the British Empire was drawing profits out of India while hundreds of millions of Indians lived in misery, many threatened by famine. For years, Gandhi had been leading protests. They were growing bigger, and by 1930, many expected the nonviolent leader to focus his movement on the pillars of British colonial power, perhaps the stock exchange in Bombay or the viceroy's mansion in Delhi. Instead, Gandhi chose salt.

The British monopolized the market for salt. They prohibited Indians from gathering the mineral on their own shores, forcing them to buy more expensive salt produced by British manufacturers. This was unjust. Had people in Britain, and all the other great powers, known about the monopoly, many would have been outraged. The trick was to engineer a scene most likely to bring shame thundering down on India's colonial rulers, the British Raj. So Gandhi announced that he would lead a 240-mile march to a coastal town on the Arabian Sea. On that beach, the Indians would reclaim salt, an ingredient fundamental to both cooking and health.

Gandhi's choice of salt was genius. It made it abundantly clear that the Indians were not motivated by greed or status. They were asking only for a basic element of life. Who could deny it to them? The Salt March was a perfectly designed scenario for punching up. Gandhi vowed that it would "shake the British Empire at its very foundation."

His strategy hinged on the diffusion of information. If news of the march didn't reach Britain and the rest of the Western world, the campaign would accomplish nothing. Like a falling tree in a deserted forest, shame makes no impact if its message misses its audience. And Gandhi controlled no newspaper or radio station. He had no Twitter account.

But he had a knack for attracting worldwide attention. A contingent of the international press corps followed him for the twenty-four-day march. They sent photos of him dressed in his homespun garb, speaking in villages along the way about equality and self-sufficiency. With each stop he honed his attacks on Britain, painting the overlords as rapacious and—importantly— hypocritical to their own democratic rules of conduct.

Shared values, as always, were crucial. If the target—in this case Britain—hadn't cared about its reputation for human rights, and didn't pride itself as a paragon of Western civilization, it would have been impervious to news stories detailing its exploitation of impoverished Indians. But the British, far more than Nigeria's president or Saudi Arabia's crown prince, treasured their standing as a beacon of democracy. The values they shared, or claimed to share, with Gandhi's marchers made them vulnerable.

At first, the British showed restraint. They understood the punching-up game. They didn't interfere when Gandhi, in front of a massive crowd, had his triumphant moment. Reaching down, he grabbed a fist-sized lump of salt from the beach and held it high over his head for the cameras. There was minimal response from the government. He quickly upped the stakes and announced plans to lead a popular takeover of the salt company. That's when the colonial government threw him in jail—tarnishing Britain's global reputation.

While Gandhi was in jail, some 2,500 of his followers marched to those saltworks, instigating an extreme version of punching up. Police attacked them, striking their heads with wooden bats. The Indians, committed to nonviolence, did not even lift their arms to defend themselves, thereby leaving no room for alternate narratives that blamed them for the conflict. According to an American journalist who witnessed the scene, "They went down like ten-pins."

The drama played out much as Gandhi had designed it, with the Indian protesters appearing saintly while the empire and its forces behaved like brutes for all the world to see. In the U.S. Congress, accounts of the Salt March violence were read into the record, and opposition to Britain's rule in India grew. It also fed anti-colonialism in Britain. Winston Churchill later admitted that Gandhi's salt campaign had "inflicted such humiliation and defiance as has not been known since the British first trod the soil of India."

Shame clearly worked as a battering ram against injustice, even when the shamers took a physical beating. Many of them came from lower castes. Over the centuries, they had been told in countless ways that they were inferior and deserved their lowly station in life. If they spoke out about their oppression, whether in terms of education, housing, or even salt, they faced ridicule. They were uneducated, their diet was ungodly, they spoke funny. Most of them were locked, voiceless, in the first stage of shame. How could such lowly creatures dare to claim the rights of citizenship and equality?

This was classic punching down, the kind we've seen in the treatment of people with addictions and the poor. And it was crucial for Gandhi (and later, his American disciple Martin Luther King, Jr.) to inspire his followers with pride so that they could stand up to their oppressors. To this end, Gandhi made a point of bathing with the so-called untouchables, known today as the Dalit. He preached that poverty was nothing to be ashamed of. Instead, they should be proud of their simple and virtuous existence, as well as their beauty and dignity as human beings.

Gandhi and his supporters were using shame to attack the system that was holding them down and silencing them. But it's important to note that the process, as is often the case, was excruciatingly slow. It would be another seventeen years before India's punching-up campaign achieved its ultimate goal of ending British rule in the subcontinent.

Punching up results in all kinds of discomfort and anxiety, even among supporters of a cause. The battle for civil rights, it turns out, is rarely civil. As its name implies, punching up is an aggressive and provocative act. It can hurt people. It can disgust them. Some will inevitably complain that the shamers have gone too far.

Larry Kramer, the writer and AIDS activist, took his punching-up campaign to levels of nastiness and acrimony that even his allies found alarming. In 1981, as the AIDS epidemic was just starting to ravage gay communities, Kramer cofounded the Gay Men's Health Crisis. The idea was to draw attention and resources to the plague, even if it meant pelting opponents with condoms or stenciling bloody handprints on walls. Such aggressive tactics alienated Kramer's fellow members. They kicked him out, and he in turn called them "sissies."

Kramer was just getting started. His next venture, ACT UP (AIDS Coalition to Unleash Power), launched vitriolic attacks on the political and medical establishments, which still regarded AIDS as "only" a gay problem (and, consequently, shamed the victims for making bad choices). Kramer was relentless and caustic in his moral crusade to push resources toward AIDS research and therapeutics. In 1988, a year before he tested positive for the virus, he wrote an open letter to Dr. Anthony Fauci, who was already directing the National Institute of Allergy and Infectious Diseases:

> *I have been screaming at the National Institutes of Health since I first visited your Animal House of Horrors in 1984. I called you monsters then and I called you idiots in my play, The Normal Heart, and now I call you murderers.*
>
> *You are responsible for supervising all government-funded AIDS treatment research programs. In the name of right, you make decisions that cost the lives of others. I call that murder.*

Many of Kramer's allies thought this was excessive, that he was rude, ungrateful, a loudmouth, but his shaming campaign turned out to be effective. It framed the response to HIV as a moral choice. It prompted a surge of research that eventually saved thousands upon thousands of lives (including his own). As Kramer himself said in 1995, "If you write a calm letter and fax it to nobody, it sinks like a brick in the Hudson."

For many people, especially those without much power, incivility is the only tool at their disposal. On a June evening in 2018, the target was Sarah Huckabee Sanders, the pugnacious White House press secretary. When she and a few friends stopped for dinner at a small upscale restaurant, the Red Hen, in Lexington, Virginia, the restaurant staff was unhappy to see her. From their perspective, she represented an inhumane government, one that discriminated against transgender people, incited violence in American cities, and separated mothers from their children on the Mexican border, among other atrocities. Sanders, they believed, not only defended these policies but also lied about them on a regular basis. They didn't want to serve her.

So the co-owner of the Red Hen, Stephanie Wilkinson, took Sanders to one side and quietly explained to her that she had to go. Sanders accepted this decision calmly and left with her husband. The other six people, who were already eating their appetizers, were invited to stay. But they left too. The appetizers, Wilkinson told them, were on the house.

Nestled in Virginia's Shenandoah Valley, Lexington is an iconic town for Civil War buffs, especially fans of the losing side. The Confederacy's legendary generals, Robert E. Lee and Thomas "Stonewall" Jackson, are buried there. For decades after the war, the town hewed to Jim Crow laws, maintaining segregated schools, neighborhoods, and cemeteries. If a Black woman in those times had dared to sit in one of Lexington's restaurants for whites, she would no doubt have received the same treatment as Sarah Sanders. Someone would have told her to leave, perhaps in a quiet voice, or maybe more forcefully. But it would have been a shaming experience either way.

There's a crucial difference between the two expulsions. One person is shamed for what she does; the other for what she is. A Black woman who had the effrontery—or courage—to step into that restaurant in the 1950s could not choose her race. Restaurants denied service to Blacks not for what they said or how they behaved but for who they were. Sarah Sanders, by contrast, had a choice. She could choose to tell the truth or quit her job. That is the first distinguishing mark of punching-up targets. The second is their degree of power. Sarah Sanders was at the time the spokesperson for the White House. By any standard, she had the wherewithal to defend her lies and complain about the unfairness of her treatment. Compare her position to that of the untold number of

Black families denied service in restaurants and hotels whose complaints were ignored.

Punching up can only happen when there's a choice, and when there's a voice. And when it works, the people with power adjust their behavior. They start to make different and better choices.

After leaving the restaurant that night, Sanders tweeted about her ouster. And the news promptly gained a life of its own in the media. It sparked the expected indignation on Fox News and in the conservative blogosphere. This was no surprise. Yet some who shared the Red Hen's views about Sanders were also unhappy. David Axelrod, Barack Obama's former senior adviser, said he was "amazed and appalled" by the lack of civility. *The Washington Post* editorial page appealed for comity in a time of angry polarization, writing that Sanders, whatever her faults, "should be allowed to eat dinner in peace."

You could make a case against the Red Hen's decision. It turned off moderates while providing Sanders's allies with self-righteous talking points, which fit neatly into fundraising pitches. But the punching up in this case was less political than moral. It wasn't a purely partisan play. Sarah Sanders, as the executive branch's chief spokesperson, was creating a dangerous new standard for bald-faced lies and obfuscation. The restaurateurs fought against it with their only weapon at hand, punching-up shame.

Kids are the very best shamers—in part because it's so much harder to accuse them of incivility. They embody innocence and hope, and they rarely have any skin in the game, whether power or money, so their motives are pure. They have only their values. A perfect example is Greta Thunberg, the Swedish teenager who in 2018 launched a solitary campaign to shame polluters and save the planet from global warming. She mobilized student strikes around the globe. Attempts to shame her, including mocking tweets from the White House and efforts to graft her image onto pornography, fell flat and made those doing it look desperate and immoral.

Following a murderous attack on a Parkland, Florida, school in 2018, young survivors there launched a similar punching-up campaign, Never Again MSD. These grieving students from Marjory Stoneman Douglas High School had escaped death, some by hiding in closets, others simply out of the line of fire. But seventeen of their classmates and teachers were dead. Never Again MSD shamed governors and legislators for refusing to enact gun control (while accepting big contributions from the gun lobby). The charismatic activists got loads of attention, on TV and from Democrats in Congress and state legislatures. They were featured on the cover of *Time* magazine.

The shamed politicians and their supporters fought back: They denigrated the students, accusing them of opportunism and secretly taking money from liberal groups. This is the age-old response to punching up. If the image of righteous protesters can be sullied or their motives questioned, they lose their perceived virtue and shed their claim to moral authority.

Laura Ingraham of Fox News ridiculed one of the student leaders, David Hogg, on Twitter, for being rejected by four universities he'd applied to and "whining" about it. Hogg promptly responded by tweeting a list of twelve advertisers on Ingraham's show, urging his followers to shame them. A day later, a chastened Ingraham backtracked: "On reflection, in the spirit of Holy Week, I apologize for any upset or hurt my tweet caused [Hogg] or any of the brave victims of Parkland." By that point, companies including Wayfair and Tripadvisor had already pulled their ads from her show. Hogg's punching up worked. (But predictably, it infuriated gun rights supporters. One of them, responding to his tweet, wrote: "@davidhogg111 is the real bully here! Shame!!")

Two months after the school shooting, the students organized a "die-in" at a Publix supermarket. The chain had donated more than $600,000 to a gubernatorial candidate, Adam Putnam, who bragged about his top rating (and financial support) from the National Rifle Association.

Hogg tweeted:

In Parkland we will have a die in the Friday (the 25th) before memorial day weekend. . . . Just go an lie down starting at 4. Feel free to die in with us at as many other @Publix as possible.

The supermarket forestalled these shaming events by renouncing further political contributions. On a larger scale, the Parkland students triggered a national protest movement, one that spread to young people (and their parents) all over the country. Protests turned into voter-registration efforts. Like Nigeria's anti-SARS mobilization, the student activists from Florida began by shaming one target, the gun lobby. But the energy and focus quickly broadened to issues of social justice.

In the summer of 2017, the #MeToo movement exploded onto the scene. It was ignited by journalistic exposés of Harvey Weinstein, a power broker and predator who used his clout in Hollywood to stake his claim, often violently, to virtually any woman in the industry who struck his fancy. And since this was Hollywood, a magnet for human beauty, potential victims popped up everywhere Weinstein went.

Weinstein's abuses were horrific. But what is especially noteworthy, and tragic, about his case is that his crimes were an open secret in Hollywood. Everybody knew someone, or knew someone who knew someone, who had a story to tell. Even so, it remained stubbornly under wraps, a violently misogynistic status quo.

Shame, of course, played a role in this silence. Like many victims

of sexual crimes, the women Weinstein raped or coerced naturally found it hard to discuss. People would always murmur that
these women had asked for it, that they were sleeping with him to
advance their career, that they could have said no. The women were
also painfully aware that if they spoke out, they could find themselves starved for work, on an informal blacklist of troublemakers.
They'd seen it happen to Rose McGowan, one of the few who had
dared to speak out about Weinstein's sexual assault. It was as if he,
along with his enablers, his handlers, and his top-dollar lawyers,
held his female victims in a cage.

The sexual shaming of women is as old as the Bible. What was
new and wildly disorienting for many was what broke out in the
wake of the Weinstein exposé. It was the sexual shaming of men.

Powerful men had long paid lip service to gender equity and
respect for women in the workplace. Corporate titans and network chieftains made generous donations to shelters for battered
women. They festooned headquarters with pink ribbons for breast
cancer awareness. Yet they remained free to behave, with varying
levels of circumspection, like pigs. That was the way things worked,
and it was based on deeply entrenched hierarchies.

The change came practically overnight. Women, silenced
through the ages about the abuses they endured, suddenly gained
their voices. With social media, they could broadcast their denunciations. And now they were (mostly) believed. Their virtue was not
questioned (or at least not as much). Rules of decency were now
enforceable. The cultural gatekeepers in the country, from the TV
networks to Fortune 500 companies, climbed aboard the #MeToo
movement. Predators were fired. The old order was turned on its
head. The punching-up campaign was registering results.

What followed was a torrent of lurid and disturbing accusations:
If norms can be seen as tectonic plates, these were earthquakes of

shame that moved them with massive force. As their façade was torn away, men saw their shining reputations in tatters. Charlie Rose, the genial television talk show host, was accused of circulating among female colleagues stark naked and groping their breasts or any other part of their bodies his hands settled on. Several women charged that the comedian Louis C.K. had forced them to watch him masturbate. Matt Lauer, the co-host of NBC's *Today* show, was said to have a button under his desk that would lock his office door, presumably to shut off the escape route for his female victims. These alleged perpetrators faced shame on an epic scale.

Within weeks, there was a vast culling of men behaving badly. More than two hundred entertainers, executives, and politicians (both state and national) were forced to resign for pinching, pawing, propositioning, or demeaning women, making off-color jokes, posting naked pictures of exes on Instagram—the list goes on. After marching through their lives with the assurance that society's sexual mores were fashioned in their favor, powerful men were finally being held to account. For many who had long basked in status and privilege, it was scary. They lawyered up and issued abject apologies, often while denying the felonious details. They found themselves scrambling to escape professional and social banishment, and in some cases, prison.

These shifting norms were bound to drive many men into the second stage of shame—stirring their rage and denial and recriminations. After all, even if their behavior was immature, boorish, even hateful, many could claim that they were playing by the largely unwritten rules as they knew them. Their overnight transformation from role models to scum was a recipe for cognitive dissonance.

A year after the awakening of the #MeToo movement, *Châtelaine,* a Canadian women's magazine, surveyed one thousand men on the topic of sexual harassment. Fully one-quarter of the respondents were neutral on the subject. But of the remaining three-quarters, 46 percent felt either angry, guilty, or persecuted. In the comments, one man's fallacious argument oozed with misplaced grievance. "I feel bad for the [women] who have actually had it happen to them, but also persecuted by those who just want attention."

It's easy to see where the men's discomfort came from. For the first time, they weren't in control. With #MeToo, women found themselves newly empowered to shame them. And this quickly extended from men's actions to their words—what they said, wrote, or tweeted. A man could have drinks with dinner, disappear into the bathroom with his phone, and stumble out minutes later having deep-sixed his career with a toxic tweet.

One case among many is that of Stuart Baker, a voice actor on the animated series, *Squidbillies*. Combining his animus toward the movements for both race and gender equity, he lambasted Dolly Parton in a Facebook post for embracing Black Lives Matter. "So now this freak-titted old Southern bimbo is a BLM lover? Remember, slut, Rednecks made you a Millionaire!"

The next day, desperate to salvage his livelihood, he issued a parody of shame, positioning himself as a victim. "[I] sincerely apologize for my post regarding Dolly Parton, BLM, race and everything. I apologized for my actions, my bad choice of words and any offense I may have caused to anyone. I don't know what else you want from me. If you're not satisfied with my apology, just tell me what else you want."

When he was fired and vilified across social media, he sought refuge within a like-minded bubble, among people who agreed with his original posting. This freed him to lash out at this group's common enemies and reiterate even more forcefully the same message that had sunk his career.

I just hope you a--holes are happy you took a good Man and talent down. You succeeded. Be proud that you ruined a person's life all because of [the] Freak Show called "Dolly Parton and BLM." Thanks a lot. I gave my best to you assholes for over 30 years. I guess you just love to kick someone when they're down. That's so twisted and perverted. Again, thanks! I'm remember[ing] you bastards!

This is the messy untangling that accompanies rapid change. Each side shames the other, at times overzealously. For men in the mainstream, a new understanding backed up by the punishing force of shame is pushing a great number of them toward the new norms—in this case, accountability for their treatment of women. Some embrace them. Others, like Stuart Baker, grumble. They don't have to search too hard to find examples where the shamers seem to take it too far. Opponents use these cases to discredit the entire movement.

Meanwhile, great numbers of white men look on from the sidelines. Overt harassment is lamentable, of course. But they don't see themselves as responsible. They don't demean women, much less coerce them for sex. Yet many of these men remain stuck in the denial stage. They haven't yet come to grips with both the power they wield in sustaining a status quo built upon injustice and the benefits they reap from it.

To be fair, this kind of cognitive dissonance is an issue for all of us. But those who benefit the most have the greatest responsibility to advance from a state of denial to accepting responsibility and pushing for justice.

Today's titans of shame, the ones controlling the lion's share of the machinery, are trillion-dollar digital platforms, most notably

Google and Facebook. As we've seen, they track and target us, tag us with digital scarlet letters, and feed us the bits of information, truth or fiction, most likely to juice their bottom lines. These systems are invasive and biased. The steady accumulation of their misdeeds has unleashed waves of shame directed their way. That raises the frightening specter of regulation, and it has led them to take baby steps toward accountability. Yet the only way to lay bare what they're up to, and change it, is to dig through the artificial intelligence engines that power them. This requires the deepest technical expertise.

Google, for one, worked to boost its fairness credentials in 2018 when it hired Timnit Gebru from Microsoft. Born in Ethiopia, Gebru had a PhD in AI from Stanford. Alongside MIT researcher Joy Buolamwini and computer whiz Deborah Raji, she had published a groundbreaking 2017 study showing how facial recognition software, developed largely from images of white people, was 99 percent accurate in identifying white males but only 65 percent accurate when it came to Black women. So if a camera picked up the face of a Black woman at a crime scene, the system would likely match it to a large number of innocent people. These disturbing findings led Amazon and Microsoft to stop selling the software to law enforcement.

In 2020, Gebru and her growing team at Google turned their attention to the biases of "immense language models"—the raw material for much of Google's AI. The paper—"On the Dangers of Stochastic Parrots: Can Language Models Be Too Big?"—worked to establish the statistical likelihood that racism and other biases would be embedded in Google's automated services. The paper suggested, pointedly, that more culturally sensitive models could be developed by directing the machine learning on more focused data sets. In other words, Google could reduce the unfairness in its information empire if it wanted to. The tacit conclusion, painful to

Google, was that if it chose not to revamp its spectacularly profitable status quo, it was choosing to be racist.

The paper went through internal review and seemed poised for publication. But five weeks later, in late November 2020, Google ordered Gebru to withdraw it, citing a lack of context, including countervailing research. She refused and punched up hard. In an email to her colleagues, she denounced the company for censoring her, for brushing off the bias issues that she and her team had highlighted, and for lagging in efforts to hire minorities. Google fired her.

Gebru's response was to turn her firing into a shaming event. She shared her experience widely on social media. The tech giant, she said in interviews, was happy to bask in praise for hiring an AI luminary—and an African woman to boot—to ferret bias from its system. But her advice was less welcome.

This punching-up campaign, like others, shamed the target for betraying its principles. In Google's case, the values in question were clear for all to see. In the prospectus for its 2004 public stock offering, the Google founders had inserted, a bit ostentatiously, a clause in which they vowed to distinguish themselves morally from their money-grubbing competitors.

Don't be evil. We believe strongly that in the long term, we will be better served—as shareholders and in all other ways—by a company that does good things for the world even if we forgo some short term gains. This is an important aspect of our culture and is broadly shared within the company.

This lofty promise made the company especially vulnerable to Gebru's damning charges. More than two thousand employees at Google promptly signed a petition denouncing her firing. It

demanded a thorough explanation of the process by the leaders of
the research division and a stronger commitment by the company
to "research integrity and academic freedom."

A week later, Sundar Pichai, chief executive of Google's parent
company, Alphabet, issued an apology:

> I've heard the reaction to Dr. Gebru's departure loud and clear: It
> seeded doubts and led some in our community to question their
> place at Google. I want to say how sorry I am for that, and I accept
> the responsibility of working to restore your trust.

But the struggle continued. Less than three months after Gebru's dismissal, one of her top collaborators, Margaret Mitchell, was
let go. Mitchell, also on the ethical AI team, had encouraged Gebru
two years earlier to join her at Google. Outraged by the firing, she
had written a detailed denunciation and circulated it on Twitter.
Each small problem, she wrote, referring to her work at the company, "expands into a vast universe of new complex problems." She
called untangling bias from Google's universe of AI the "infinite
onion." The issues ranged from fairness to freedom and equality.

It was shortly after Gebru was sacked, sources told the press,
that Google zeroed in on Mitchell's online activity. She seemed to
be searching her emails for information relating to Gebru's time at
the company—a sign that she might be building a case against the
firm. Mitchell was suspended, and a month later, on February 19,
2021, she posted a two-word tweet: "I'm fired."

Google has a lot to lose. The company's future hinges on recruit-
ing and retaining the very best minds. These luminaries have their
choice of laboratories, from Facebook and Amazon and venture-
funded start-ups, to the most prestigious universities. What they
hunger for are discoveries, breakthroughs. Freedom is essential for
this. And if they don't believe they can work unfettered at Google,

they'll go elsewhere. In the field of AI, a brain drain is an existential threat.

In attempting to muzzle Gebru, the company, arguably, betrayed its original promise not to sacrifice its principles for short-term gain. Now, as employees continue to shame Google for its behavior, it may end up concluding that the best way to keep them happy, and retain its allure as a top research hub, is to follow its original anti-evil mandate—or at least take a step or two in that direction. Researchers, after all, tend to be more zealous about academic freedom than profits.

Punching up within these technology platforms could hardly be more crucial. The decisions these companies make as they deploy ever more sophisticated and invasive AI into our lives will be fundamental to our welfare and democracy. The shaming campaigns to corral them, to hold them to their loftiest promises, and to reorient their power toward the common good will be the work of a generation, or maybe longer.

The fired-up PhDs in the Google campaign are in a strong position, with more leverage than the Nigerian masses in the anti-SARS movement or the restaurant owner who told Sarah Sanders to eat elsewhere. They are at the controls of the world's richest industry. Their skills are essential. When even one of them punches up, it can hurt. We can only hope that more of them find their voice.

CHAPTER 10

UNDER THE KNIFE

f you had asked me in, say, 2015, how I felt about being fat, I would have used the opportunity to demonstrate my enlightenment on the issue. I believed that I was finally comfortable being heavy, certainly not a vocal activist about it, but a good way past the lacerating shame I'd endured for decades. I even considered myself a role model for people trying to accept their bodies. I understood that a considerable determinant of body size is genetic. There were myriad theories to explain the global obesity epidemic, and the marketplace was teeming with therapies and elixirs. But none provided answers for me. Being fat wasn't my choice and I wasn't particularly interested in discussing it.

My priority at the time was not to lose weight but instead to lower my risk factors for diabetes, a disease I had seen ruin my father's health. My plan was to eat nutritious food and get plenty of exercise. I had not yet come to terms with the stages of shame. But if you'd described them to me, back then, I would have placed myself solidly in the third stage. I was making my way out of shame, trying to embrace the body I had.

However, all the inner peace in the world counts for next to nothing when you're fat, approaching middle age, and struggling mightily to stay in shape by biking on hilly terrain in ninety-five-degree summer heat. My body couldn't take it, and I abandoned my workouts. In the following months, as I spent more time inside, unwilling to leave the air-conditioned cool of my home, my blood sugar level inched up into the dangerous prediabetic range. My dad had gotten diagnosed with diabetes at my age, and my brother, older than me by two years, had just gotten the bad news. I had all the risk factors except I exercised, but now I was losing that battle as well. I didn't want diabetes, but it was beginning to feel inevitable.

I understood by then that diets failed, usually within a year. This fed the weight-loss industry with endless chains of repeat customers. It was their business model. And they enticed people, like other shame industries, with pseudoscience and miracle cures. That much I knew. To confront my diabetes threat, I had to turn away from the hucksters. I needed answers from sources I could believe.

For me, that meant science.

Science is by no means perfect. There are still plenty of abuses—researchers out to make a buck, papers published with shoddy statistical analysis, the lowly and vindictive politics of research universities, and the silly rivalries. Still, science by definition has rigor. People (often, not always!) get called on bullshit. They are eventually pushed to defend their position with data. If we're looking for answers about how our systems work—whether it's the shape of our bodies or the vulnerabilities of a virus—peer-reviewed science with double-blind experiments is the best source we have.

I had something to go on. A news article I'd read had described bariatric surgery as a near cure for type II diabetes. Its efficacy shocked the experts, because it seemed to function almost as an off button for the elevated blood sugars that cause the condition. In fact, even patients who didn't successfully lose weight after the bariatric surgery—normally considered a weight-loss procedure—still recovered from diabetes.

Why wasn't it called a diabetes surgery that had weight-loss side effects, instead of the reverse? I think about that often.

I'm guessing it's because weight loss is a mass market with tens of millions of customers hungry for miracles—and an escape from shame. There's less money to be made curing diabetes.

When I searched on Google for research on bariatric surgery, I was immediately inundated by advertising come-ons, trying to shame me into buying a silver bullet. Lurid before-and-after pictures, plastic surgery promotions, and quick-fix promises filled my feed. Science was clearly overwhelmed by the fat-shame industry, at least in the commercial space that is the modern internet. Sifting credible nuggets from the mountains of hype and profiteering pseudoscience was an ordeal. It also triggered my fat fears and anxieties. Each time I tried to do research, I ended up questioning my choices and my worthiness.

Fortunately, I had access to the online libraries at Columbia University and was able to consult peer-reviewed studies on weight-loss surgeries. There I was able to follow the progression of the science. The first approach, late in the twentieth century, was Lap-Band surgery, where they placed a big rubber band around the patient's stomach and squeezed it, effectively making it smaller. But the effects didn't last long.

Researchers studied different approaches on both mice and humans. What they found was that the gut biome—the mixture of microbes that creates its own chemical environment in the stomach—did not change much with Lap-Band surgery. Despite the disruption, the metabolically active stomach cells continued to emit hormones and, crucially, signal hunger. Patients regained weight.

So I began to focus more on something called the bariatric sleeve procedure. This involves surgery removing the stretchy tissue of the stomach and then stitching the rest back up. It results in a shrunken organ the shape of a banana. One particularly impressive study focused on how the operation changed the mice's biomes.* It found that after the procedure, the gut biomes of the formerly fat mice were much closer to the biomes of skinny mice.

I interviewed half a dozen women who had undergone bariatric sleeve, some recently and others many years earlier. They told me about problems, especially the risks of vitamin deficiency. The shrunken stomach cannot absorb certain key vitamins without help, which is why patients must take vitamins every day for the rest of their lives. None of these women, however, had regrets. One of them, who had the surgery in her seventies, only felt remorse for not having it sooner.

I decided to go for it. And why not? I had excellent health insurance. Living in Manhattan, I had access to world-class medical facilities. NewYork-Presbyterian Hospital, where I'd have my surgery, was just a ten-minute subway ride north.

The challenge, though, would be to convince my insurer to pay for it. Elsewhere, this is not so hard. Since it is extremely effective as a treatment for diabetes, bariatric surgery has been adopted widely in the United Kingdom, where people can qualify for it just by having a large enough body mass index (BMI). It is also gaining popularity in Israel. The savings for the national health systems were realized within a few years, because one surgery cost less than decades of managing two chronic conditions, obesity and diabetes, as well as hip and knee replacements brought on by carrying the excess weight.

You'd think the same logic would extend to the United States. But it doesn't. While it's true that the expensive surgery, running

---

*The more extreme gastric bypass surgery reroutes the tubing, bypassing the shrunken stomach altogether.

from $15,000 to $30,000, saves money in the long run, insurance companies see financial risk. What happens if they pay for the surgery only to see a newly healthy post-bariatric customer jumping to a different insurer or Medicare? That insurer would then have invested in the person's health without reaping any rewards.

Not surprisingly, my insurer put up stiff resistance. Getting clearance for the surgery was a six-month ordeal. I took it on as a second part-time job. It involved filling out countless forms, not to mention hunting down doctors and hounding them to testify that I badly needed the surgery. The tyranny of paperwork was absolute. I had to provide five separate years of medical records just to prove that I'd been fat for a long time. And these years, they stipulated, could not include any of my pregnant time (I'd had three kids). Fat while pregnant didn't count. They were inflexible on that issue, among many others.

I had to make numerous calls to doctors who had treated me more than a decade earlier, in grad school. Getting doctors' offices to find, copy, and send ancient forms requires endless time and a constant flow of "friendly" nudges and reminders. I spent entire days on the phone, begging, cajoling, and sweet-talking people into digging through dusty old records (sometimes still on paper!) and faxing them to me.*

The process separately demanded monthly visits—six of them!—to my doctor, and mandated that he put me on a "last-ditch diet." He did so, and shortly thereafter wrote a required sad-sack letter to my insurance company saying that I was morbidly obese and uncurable by traditional methods, that I'd tried and flubbed multiple diets and could reasonably be considered desperate. Only with that stamp of shame could I qualify.

---

*Critical question, after being utterly polite: "What would you do if you were me?"

This colossal and, at times, degrading hassle brought to mind the bureaucratic roadblocks and shaming that people face when applying for food stamps or welfare. It involves not only documenting your weaknesses but also making a compelling case that they are all too real, and unresolvable. These shame machines demand groveling. I was deeply humiliated. I persisted only because I was able to see through my pain to the machine's inner workings. I was adamant that I wouldn't be cowed by intentional, profit-driven shaming.

Eventually, I got the go-ahead from the insurer. A few weeks later, after a grueling pre-op diet to shrink my fatty liver, I went to the hospital, overnight bag in hand, to have my stomach surgically shrunk.

I worried that I'd left the hospital too quickly after the operation. In the cab, each bump was brutal. This brought home the often ignored reality of surgery: its violence. Someone had cut into my body, carved out half of my stomach, and sewed it up with what felt like twine.

Once back in my house, I followed the meticulous recovery diet (mostly water the first week) and at the same time dealt with my incessant pain by swallowing Tylenol laced with codeine every six hours. Early on, I hated with a vengeance the smell and taste. But it's funny—and horrifying—how quickly you can get used to it, and want more. I threw out the medicine when I saw that I was starting to truly crave it, and even enjoy its taste.

My body took time to heal, but the surgery was a success. I lost a good amount of weight (although I'm still fat) and was able to exercise again, even in the summer heat. My blood sugar numbers improved, as promised, and the threat of diabetes receded. I take my vitamins twice a day, knowing how I could be debilitated if I don't.

After I went through the surgery, I lost my sweet tooth. My favorite food went from ice cream to brussels sprouts, and bitter things were much more delicious. I craved roasted vegetables for the first time in my life. And, retroactively, I realized that "skinny food"—food that skinny people seemed to like—was much more an indulgence than I had ever imagined. The key, apparently, is having the right gut biome in your stomach. I will never again feel bad about craving chocolate or more virtuous than others for eating vegetables. We are all just doing what our bodies are asking us to do.

So, I could spin this into the triumphant story of a fat woman who spent much of her life immersed in shame but managed to come to grips with the dark forces at play—a woman who disregarded the false and frantic promises of the fat-shame machine. Looking instead to science, she confronted the problem and overcame it.

I wish it were that simple. Sadly, shame accompanied me on every step of the journey, and it hasn't gone away. Bariatric surgery, after all, operates within the shame industry. For all of its scientific virtues, it accepts the prevailing premises that have proven so lasting and profitable for dieting companies, the very same illusions and phobias. It also propagates them. They're essential to its business model.

Even the slightest reminder of weight issues brings alive fat shame and self-questioning. Once shame inhabits you, especially from a young age, it's with you for the long haul. You can keep it at bay and win important battles. But it's forever out there, probing your defenses, angling to get back in and run the show. It poses the same demoralizing question on a loop: You can't really feel good about yourself, can you?

The trouble starts with the choice to undergo surgery, which itself stirs shame. Most of us have been told our entire lives that winners pursue their goals and achieve them. Losers quit. And if you've pulled the plug on eight or ten diets and your attic is jammed with unused exercise machines, if you've been to a fat farm or two and participate actively on a Facebook page about dieting, if you've done all that and you're still as fat as ever—then you're a loser.

Submitting to the knife is seen as the ultimate surrender. If you don't hear a lot about bariatric surgery, it's because most people keep it to themselves. They're ashamed. I was sad but not surprised when an obese friend of mine told me she'd never get the operation because she wanted to lose weight "the real way."

Fat shame mixed with pseudoscience pervades even the hospitals. One day I was sitting in the waiting room of my surgeon, at NewYork-Presbyterian Hospital in Manhattan, for a follow-up appointment. I overheard my surgeon in the next room talking to the secretary across the hall about a new diet he was on. He had bought the bestseller *Eat Fat, Get Thin*, and was very excited about it.

So even my chosen scientific practitioner at the world-class research hospital was buying into the thriving branch of the shame industry built upon phony diet science. How could an ordinary person be expected to transcend this, especially if they don't have access to scientific journals or the education (and patience) to read and understand them?

After the surgery, I returned for regular follow-up appointments, where I met a very friendly nurse practitioner named Gio. With a broad and encouraging smile, he would ask me at the beginning of every meeting what my target weight was. It was the first thing he said after hello. In other words, how thin do you plan to get? What number are you shooting for? Once Gio had my information, he would add it to a chart he was making for me. And together, we could track my weight-loss progress, every few weeks, toward my ultimate goal.

At first, I played the game. I wanted this to work. I wanted to lose weight. Along with the others in my group, I shed pounds, and the line on my chart trended down, pointing to success. As it did, I had flashbacks to my parents' weekly weigh-ins and graphs and those fleeting moments of euphoria that I'd experienced on my first diet. It was exciting and triggering at the same time.

I was hardly alone. Each of us in the post-op bariatric group had been grappling most of our lives with losing weight. We had experienced the heady rush of early dieting, when the pounds come off and the chart looks fabulous—a dream come true—and later the crushing disappointment as that target weight recedes with each pound regained.

And here we were, reenacting the exact same scene. I assured myself that this time would be different, because I wasn't hungry! That lifted my hopes that bariatric surgery would live up to its billing, that the benefits would last, that I would be thin (or at least much thinner) for the rest of my (longer) life.

Nevertheless, the target number brought shame into the equation. As soon as a number is established, any deviation from it is deemed failure. And I'll admit that even with all of my awareness of shame, and my pride at having overcome the worst of it, I fell headlong into the target-weight drama. This created cognitive dissonance. I had learned to manage shame, or so I thought. Yet I was being managed by it, like I was eleven years old again.

Instead of shrinking to a target number, my fellow patients and I might have focused on gaining mobility. If I felt more energy and could ride my bike twenty miles on a hot summer day, that would be a big step forward. Another plus would be if my blood sugar number dropped into a safe range. The goal was to reclaim my movement and my health. If I ended up plateauing ten or twenty pounds above my so-called target weight, so what?

I knew that much, rationally speaking. The trouble is that once you have that number on the chart, it has its way with your feelings and defines your self-worth. For the tiny minority that actually reaches a target weight and holds on to it, it must feel like a proud achievement. But for the vast majority of us, it's never-ending disappointment and pain.

After the first few meetings, when Gio asked for my target weight, I would explain my objections to him, sparing no details. Target weights, I said, are insidious promoters of shame. I thought he understood, but the next visit he would ask me, first thing, for my target weight. He would never change, but I kept at it.

During one appointment, Gio was accompanied by a young intern, a woman with a Muslim headscarf who was quietly taking notes. After the session, she came outside with me and thanked me for the impassioned lecture I'd just delivered on the target weight as a source of shame. Gio had barely heard it, but I'd like to think she will keep it in mind.

By rejecting the target weight, I had managed to identify one shame trigger. I was intent on banishing it. Yet even when you make a conscious decision to disarm a shame trigger, feelings don't necessarily fall into line. Institutional shame is enormously durable and persistent. Despite my impeccable reasoning, shame was still with me. Even after I threw out the scale—over the objections of my family—I continued to suspect I was missing my target weight, and I felt embarrassed. In that context, all of my sensible arguments sounded like excuses for flunking.

During this period, I felt myself confronting waves of shame, some new, others rippling from my childhood. It was silly to expect otherwise. When a fat person deals in any way with their weight, whether attempting to hide or excise it, emotions are bound to run high. To deal with this, I knew, it was important to seek out a supportive community. People need to help one another.

I considered joining the Facebook group of fellow bariatric patients that I was researching as part of this project. I lurked on the site for a few weeks. But I saw that despite good intentions, these women had bought into the expectations of the shame machine. They were swapping tips on how to slim down, and they focused, obsessively, on their ever-elusive target weight.

That single number was the group's North Star. Each person's purpose was to reach the target weight and hold on to it tight. They also went into detail discussing ways to hide the fact that they'd had bariatric surgery, so other people wouldn't think they'd "cheated."

Even success, it turned out, created problems for them. The hospitals had marketed the surgeries with extravagant promises. Instead of settling for the truth—that patients could achieve healthier weights and reduce the risk of diabetes and other diseases—they sold them dreams. The before-and-after pictures, very much like those on *The Biggest Loser,* showed obese people turning thin and shapely. This laid the groundwork for more shame, because the reality, for most of us, was short on glamour. Newly thin patients were often left with extra skin flapping about, and not all the curves in the prescribed places. That led some of them to feel bad about themselves and consider yet more surgery. Their journeys promised to be endless, because they would always find something that needed fixing. I decided not to join the group.

In the end, I never reached my target weight. Not even close. In fact I no longer remember what it was. But I ride my bike in the summer heat and lead an active lifestyle. My blood sugar levels are normal. And the emotional side? Well, I understand it a lot better than I did. But it's something I'll always be dealing with.

My lifelong struggle adds only the tiniest fragment to a bound-less mosaic. The shamescape features all of us. And above us, potent and profitable shame machines are whirring constantly. They dominate our economies and poison countless lives. My hope is that together, once we're aware of the shame around us, we can take steps to dismantle the shame machines, large and small, and improve our world.

CONCLUSION

WHEN OUR GRANDEST dreams went up in smoke, they left behind shame machines. Consider a few of the various "wars" our political leaders have declared over the past decades: the war on poverty, the war on drugs, the war on obesity. Each was launched with great fanfare and the hope that with resolute leadership, intelligence, and sufficient funds, these evils could be vanquished. If we could send a man to the moon, the thinking went, of course we could fix these scourges.

Once the complexity and cost of these problems became apparent, though, we had a change of heart. The wars initiated on behalf of victims became wars *on* them. Our grand ambitions evaporated, and look at what took their place: the rehabs and pill pushers, the punishing bureaucracies and private prisons.

When half measures fell short, or when we were simply tired of thinking about these challenges, we unloaded the brunt of the blame on the victims. After all, the logic went, the rest of society had extended a helping hand, and at great cost. We'd declared war! And these people—the fat, those suffering with addictions, and the poor—resisted our solutions. They made bad decisions. It's their fault.

It's far easier to blame than to help. The punching-down narrative fuels a species-wide ecosystem of players whose business plans are built upon these thorny problems. The worse their victims feel and the more fruitless their efforts, the richer these entities become. Return customers are golden. And each of their debacles vindicates the shame-based status quo. This narrative is easy to sell, whether for CEOs or politicians, because it seems to absolve the rest of us of responsibility for one another. It also saves money, or even better, it becomes a great way to make money on the markets: Go long on shame.

At the same time, most of us have bought into value systems that attempt to justify the rigged status quo. For those who are satisfied with their lives, it works. And those who are thriving have reason to love it. They're at the top of the ranking, and the shame machine spits out a handy explanation for their good fortune: They earned and deserve every scrap of it, thanks to good values and perseverance (abetted, of course, by enviable genes). The myth of meritocracy props them up. Others—whether through bad decisions or simple inferiority—come up disastrously short. The self-serving dichotomy that winners are good and losers bad allows us to abide deep, shame-driven inequality.

How do we confront this? Shame lurks in repressed thoughts and unspoken fear. Secrecy is its habitat, even its greenhouse. To take it on, we need truth. Only by coming face-to-face with the shame machines will we be able to dismantle them. We need a Major-League Reckoning.

One model for this is South Africa's Truth and Reconciliation Commission, which was established after the fall of apartheid in the 1990s. Throughout the country's history, and especially during the half century of apartheid, a minority of the country had repressed and abused the Black majority, jailing and killing many, while depriving an entire population of essential freedoms and virtually all opportunity.

So the South Africans talked about it. Victims were given back their voices. Ugly truths were bared. With facts verified and agreed upon, self-serving myths tended to vaporize. This learning process was necessary before society could begin to redress injustice and unfairness. You can't fix what you don't see.

Facing the truth does not guarantee a solution to problems dating back centuries, as modern South Africa can attest. But it's a necessary first step for leading populations past the first two stages of shame—hurt and denial—and into the acceptance of reality and responsibility.

To understand the situation from other perspectives, we should hold calm and nonpartisan truth and reconciliation proceedings of our own. There are signs of movement in that direction. With the rise of the #MeToo movement, women have started to emerge from shame and victimhood to tell their stories. They're testifying. And the protests following the 2020 police murder of George Floyd advanced what could become a national, and even global, discussion of race and justice. These are a promising beginning, though still far from delivering a thorough and unbiased analysis of the forces at play. Only with greater openness and disclosure will the blueprint of the shame machines come into focus. Only then will we be able to develop strategies for grinding these engines to a halt.

One way, of course, is to use shame itself, punching up at the oppressors. We see this happening already. Activists have shamed Purdue Pharma, and the Sackler family that owns it, for their role in hooking millions on opiates. This pressure, in the form of shaming protests and lawsuits, has pushed the company into bankruptcy and forced the owners to make multibillion-dollar restitutions. The family name, now stigmatized, is being scraped from the museums and university halls they funded with dirty money. It's a start.

Thanks to investigative journalism and court cases, we know enough about the Sacklers to justify punching up. Their cash cow—OxyContin—drove our addiction and suicide epidemics. We've seen the company's incriminating emails. They knew what they were doing and chose the path to shame the victims and make a fortune.

The guilty parties habitually offer their pro forma apologies, meticulously crafted by lawyers and corporate crisis consultants. It's important not to settle for these half-baked mea culpas and instead to keep punching up. A company like Purdue has tentacles reaching deep into the healthcare industry and politics. Digging into the operations of one malefactor, like Purdue, can uncover an entire network, which must be laid open and each player held accountable. The best and most honest way to bring an end to the system of crimes and mutual back-scratching is to shame the people and companies profiting from it, and to punish them with painful fines, which need to far outpace their profits. That's putting shame to good use, pushing those rich outliers to refocus on the greater good.

The next phase of our war on shame machines is to scrutinize public services, many of them funded by taxpayers. How much pain do they inflict on their poor, disadvantaged, and addicted customers? Do they shame them at every juncture? How much of the status quo is built on these dignity violations, how little on trust?

There are shame-free solutions to almost all of our social problems. For example, affordable public housing would raise the quality of life for millions, by putting a roof over their heads. That's a no-brainer. Decriminalization of drugs would keep many people out of the criminal justice system and free them from bearing the stigma of incarceration for the rest of their lives. Ending stop-and-frisk and eliminating drug tests before a person can enter a shelter would help restore dignity.

One innovative approach to addiction offers substance abusers money to visit a methadone clinic. It can be $5 on a grocery card, or $25. This element of chance and reward has the appeal of a winning poker hand. And even small dollar amounts help buy food, gas, or cigarettes. These programs are popular, and studies show that the small cash payouts work better and save more lives than traditional methods. But the idea runs against our shaming ethos, which is to punish people with an addiction until they make the right choice. So reward programs are rare. Based on their success rates and shame-free approach, they should be widespread.

Giving money to the poor, without conditions, is another potential solution. The defining problem for the poor, after all, is financial scarcity. A guaranteed basic income alleviates poverty quickly and directly. No one has to prostrate himself or herself before authorities and beg for help. We saw this work in 2020 when the U.S. government sent checks at the beginning of the pandemic, and again in features of the $1.9 trillion American Rescue Plan Act, passed in March 2021. When the entire population receives money, there's no stigma, no favoritism or special deals. And it doesn't need to cost much more than our current system; those of us who don't need the extra cash quietly funnel it back in taxes.

White shame calls for multiple reckonings, but perhaps the biggest is economic. An enormous amount of the wealth in this, the richest country in the history of the world, was created by people who were forced for centuries to work for free and then deprived of power and opportunity once liberated. A true reckoning requires reparations. And yet, the anger that this reasonable demand provokes in many quarters illustrates how, when it comes to race, most white people are stuck in a defensive and aggrieved state. Our society reflexively blames the victims, and shames them, while propagating an obscene level of economic inequality.

At the very center of this disparity is debt. It has weighed down the poor for centuries. Following the end of slavery in 1865, it was debt that maintained the status quo, shackling sharecropper families in virtual servitude. Indebtedness is not a personal failing and debtors are not to blame, which is why we should reject the language of "debt forgiveness" and instead demand debt abolition for the poor.

Our relentless ranking, rewarding winners and punishing losers, fuels this deepening inequality. Outside billionaires' condos in New York City, homeless people huddle for warmth emanating from subway grates. No college system, not even an excellent one, can make up for wildly unequal childhoods. That's why we need to start with free childcare, pre-K, and better and more equally funded school systems up to community college.

Meanwhile, the dual scourges of loneliness and distrust have mushroomed into profit centers for the social media platforms while causing widespread suffering. We've seen the loneliness of the incels and hikikomori, and the distrust fueling the anti-vaxxers and conspiracy theorists. Shaming them, it's clear, makes things worse. So what can be done to deal with the underlying problems on a systemic level?

Facebook, a mass generator of conspiracies and suspicion, is a good place to start. Already, punching-up campaigns against the company, and the resulting threats from regulators, have produced a glimmer of success. Under growing pressure, Facebook drew up goals and policy, and began to take preliminary action against misinformation. In the run-up to the 2020 U.S. presidential election, the company displayed warnings on 180 million pieces of content. It also developed an AI to detect doctored images, many of them linked to fake news. Facebook flagged some and took down others.

This was progress. But after the 2020 vote, the company eased back into the poisonous and more profitable status quo. Lies and shame, after all, drive traffic.

Such cynicism should be illegal—or prohibitively expensive. Until our government holds companies accountable, mistrust will continue to multiply. One way to push for change is to shame social media companies for lies, while also shaming politicians for

profiting from the messaging and taking related political contributions. The European Union, less in thrall to social media's influence
than the U.S. government, imposes massive fines, in the billions.
Only big numbers, and dramatic regulatory action, can change the
status quo.

Meanwhile, the pandemic plunged many of us into severe
and, for some, unbearable loneliness. This gives us an opportunity
to shine a light on efforts to address the problem. Consider the
example of Fujisato, a town in northern Japan. In the early years of
this century, the economy in the town was shrinking. The hikikomori population, at the same time, was climbing dangerously
high, reaching 9 percent of the population between eighteen and
fifty-five, or 113 people. Vosot Ikeida, an intermittent hikikomori
in Tokyo since the 1990s, writes that locals followed a counterin-
tuitive strategy. Instead of viewing the hikikomori as a problem,
they looked at them as potential solutions to their ailing economy.
In 2010, the town created so-called *ibasho*s, or places to be. They
featured ping-pong tables and board games and served tea and
sake. A few trickled outside, and others followed. Once a group of
hikikomori had ventured out to the ibashos, the organizers offered
job training in food preparation and social services. "They probably
were glad to make themselves useful," Ikeida wrote.

Five years later, eighty-six of the original hikikomori were
active in Fujisato's society. It must have felt liberating to them, as if
a thick coating of shame had melted away.

I'VE FIGURED OUT a lot over the course of this decades-long drama.
Knowledge alone cannot vanquish deep and abiding feelings and
fears. Our distant ancestors developed those adaptive emotions as
survival skills. Shame is not going away. And that's why this is not,
and could never be, a self-help book with cherry-picked examples of people recovering completely from their lifetime of shame.

Because I don't believe that's possible. Nor is it an argument that we should eradicate it, because sometimes it's our only tool against injustice.

Yet as individuals we can take action to alleviate the collective burden of inappropriate, punching-down shame and to lighten its load on the psyche of our friends and neighbors, even our species. We can brighten the lives of the people we know, including those we love, by raising our awareness of shame and applying it sensitively, and only in a way to help people return to shared norms.

Where should we start? How do we go about not inflicting unnecessary shame on others? If we could work to detoxify our relations, human life could be far more rewarding, and more peaceful. It's a big job, but we can start small.

The first step toward creating these healthier relationships is simply to look at every aspect of life through the lens of shame. This involves noticing it and labeling an interaction as shaming, whether it involves an immigration officer demeaning a refugee or a mother fat-shaming her twelve-year-old.

I have a good friend, for example, who suffered sexual abuse as a girl at the hands of a priest. She struggled, like so many others, with immense shame, as if she had been the guilty party. She shrouded it for years in secrecy. Despite this, she is still a woman of faith, now in a Protestant church. She tells me that she has friends who demean people like her for still believing in a God that would let such things happen. What these friends are doing amounts to shaming people for their religion. Yet unless these friends are looking at their behavior through the lens of shame, they probably don't see it that way. They should. We all should.

The next challenge, once shaming behavior is spotted, is to analyze it. In the case of the faith shamers, are they following a template laid out by society, or is the behavior fueled by a personal wound, a grievance, or perhaps a conversion strategy? (My friend calls them "atheist evangelists.") Are they punching down on victims of abusive priests, or punching up at the Church? Who profits from the shame, and how—either with money, status, or dominance in a relationship?

The answers may not be clear. But once such questions are percolating in our heads, we can turn them toward our own behavior. Only by creating mental inventories of the shame we emit can we refrain from poisoning people's sense of self-worth with snotty comments, ugly comparisons, judgy retweets, impossible expectations, and so on.

The first yes-no question I use to identify toxic shame is simple. Does the person have a viable choice to make? If the young Blossom Rogers we encountered earlier is addicted to crack, broke, and sleeping in her car under a bridge in Florida—does she have the choice of dressing up nicely, printing out her résumé, and applying for a receptionist job?

It's not a realistic choice. She faces an incredible amount of recovery work to recapture her voice and agency before she can get to that point. She needs to feel good about herself as a person. So for a cop to bang on Blossom's door, drag her out of the car and pin her against it, frisk her, and then dump her into the chasm of the criminal justice system represents the most vicious punching-down shame. It won't guide her toward the "right" choice. She needs help.

The second question is whether the target of shame has the power to make the necessary change. When dozens of women punched up at Miramax Films for enabling Harvey Weinstein's serial sexual predation, did the directors on the company's board have the power to fire Weinstein? Yes, they did. A corporate board, a university president, a dictator, they're all in an entirely different boat than Blossom Rogers or Joanna McCabe, the woman who tumbled off her motorized cart into the aisle at Walmart and became an online punching bag. Choice, voice, and power. If the target doesn't have them, don't we have an obligation to try a different approach?

The most important thing you can do is resist the urge to join in when people start punching down. Much of the shaming occurs online: from celebrities having a bad hair day, to people wearing inappropriate beachwear, to a right-wing high school student in an ugly staring match with a Native American elder. But it can take place at work, or in the neighborhood, or at a little-league baseball field. Someone does something wrong, and everybody feels entitled to weigh in with judgment. "You shouldn't use social media," writes journalist Ezra Klein, "to join an ongoing pile-on against a normal person."

Even assuming that the target of the shame faces a viable decision and can make a course correction, is your participation focused on improving that person's behavior, or on signaling virtue to friends? Aren't there already enough people posting that newest Karen video? Do we want her to lose her job and never find another one? Do we need to be told that openly racist behavior is racist? Aim higher, at the source of the problem. Why are the police so reliably the enforcement mechanism and private security force for white people's discomfort in the first place? Work for police reform instead of retweets.

Don't get outraged—or at least don't make a habit of it. It's true, there's more than enough to be outraged about. It's addictive. And if you want to work for prison reform or against voter repression, jump in. However, we often substitute outrage for action, because outrage feels good and appears to cost nothing. Yet it often fuels punching-down shame. When you feel outrage, examine it. Does it make you feel self-satisfied? If so, try to dial up other thoughts and emotions, and use them to make a plan for real change.

Next, consider when shame will actually be effective. You'll need the target to have a choice and a voice, but you'll also need shared norms and a sense of trust. Otherwise the shame will be bullying, ineffective, or both.

Don't shame your chubby daughter and don't go overboard with shaming your neo-Nazi son either. It is bound to backfire and leave them with fewer options in the future. By all means, talk to them about values, but focus on what they need and want, and help them make better and healthier choices for themselves. Put yourself in someone else's shoes. Extend dignity, if you have the energy and time. This helps to steer thoughts from outrage to understanding and can lead to constructive steps.

Before you hear me say "just empathize!," I should note that empathy is hardly a cure-all. It tends to embed biases, because by nature we find it easier to empathize with people like us. In *The War for Kindness,* Jamil Zaki cites cases in which white cops defend a marauding colleague, instead of reporting or shaming him, because they feel for him. Maybe they trained with him; maybe they are concerned about his family. These tribal instincts lead us to defend our own and hammer on others. The same dynamic is at work when a judicial system headed by the in-group punches down on perceived outsiders—in our case, people of color—with mass incarceration or even execution.

So empathy, while essential, cannot right social wrongs. Instead, consider a personal policy of due process. This can translate into giving people the benefit of the doubt whenever possible. Perhaps they didn't mean to do it. Perhaps it was a misunderstanding. And usually, when a person errs, nobody feels it more deeply than they do. So treat them the way you'd want others to treat you when you screw up, and respect their dignity as human beings.

Forgiveness is in many ways the flip side of shame. While shame rips open wounds, forgiveness has the power to heal them.

"Forgiveness," Nelson Mandela wrote, "liberates the soul. It removes fear. . . . That's why it's such a powerful weapon." But like empathy, it's hard and inconsistent.

As I write this, I'm thinking about a prisoner named Oscar Jones. I'd gotten to know him, because I helped to analyze the recidivism algorithms that unfairly perpetuated his decades-long confinement in federal prison. The point is not that Oscar Jones is innocent. He's not. He committed a hideous crime in the distant past. More than forty years ago, at age seventeen, he raped a woman in her seventies. He deserved to go to jail, although he was also suffering abuse at the hands of negligent caretakers. He was a peaceful inmate for the last thirty-eight years of his sentence, but after he was granted parole he was given a series of "recidivism risk" tests by the state of Illinois that deemed him likely to perpetrate further sexual crimes. That kept him incarcerated for another three years.

As an expert on algorithms and crime risk scores, I was asked by his lawyers to help them appeal this decision. One thing I noted in my letter to the court is that the test made no allowances for any progress Oscar made in prison. In other words, it permanently stigmatized him as a sexual criminal. No forgiveness from this system, ever.

After the deposition was postponed in March 2020 due to the pandemic, Oscar was diagnosed with stage IVA lung cancer. He was released in early 2021. After four decades of incarceration and scant weeks of freedom, he died on April 21, surrounded by his family. Unlike the state of Illinois, they forgave him. The unconditional and nurturing love in such a family is a healthy way to think about forgiveness and communities.

This whole process led me to wonder how we should have dealt with people like Oscar Jones, who in their youth committed a terrible crime. On the one hand, it was not my place to forgive him. I was not his victim.

On the other hand, it was my job to argue that Oscar should have been set free, and that we shouldn't have used pseudoscience to prolong his incarceration. There are, of course, powerful forces in our society that oppose this viewpoint. They want people like Oscar to stay in jail, forever tied to their crimes and out of sight. That sustains the easy dichotomy that the world is divided into good people and bad, that the bad have made bad choices, and that it's fine to keep them locked away, deprived of their humanity.

The way out of today's shamescape involves recognizing that we all make mistakes, and some of us commit crimes. We are responsible for what we do and should make amends for it. But our mistakes and missteps shouldn't plunge us into everlasting shame. There has to be an expiration date.

At its essence, detoxifying shame isn't too complicated. It involves agitating in every domain, individual as well as institutional, from the dinner table to the welfare office to the corporate boardroom, for all people to be treated with trust and dignity.

ACKNOWLEDGMENTS

SO MANY PEOPLE shared their most intimate and painful moments with me. Some of their stories are in this book, and some are not. Thank you all for your time and for your confidence.

I'm very grateful to Elizabeth Hutchinson and the kind folks of LOAS II Star Island for inviting me way back in 2019 to talk about shame and who listened so carefully, as well as everyone at Alternative Banking, Sam Smyth, and countless other people who engaged with me and allowed me to use conversations with them to work through my thinking.

I'd like to thank all the people whose writing and thinking about shame I relied on in these pages. I hope you feel I've done the topic justice. I could only draw on a fraction of the literature, but I am grateful to everyone who has explored the topic. Even if I didn't reference your work, it likely shaped my own thinking.

Finally, I'd like to thank my co-writer Steve Baker, my editor Amanda Cook, and editorial assistant Katie Berry for their incredible efforts and unreasonable trust. I'm also grateful to Sarah Breivogel, Chantelle Walker, Dan Novack, Tanvi Valsangikar, Maureen Clark, and Ada Yonenaka.

NOTES

Introduction

6 **"Unless you fly around":** "Bat Wings and the Women Who Hate Them," Blue Hare, March 4, 2021, https://blueharemagazine.com/bat-wings-women-hate.

6 **Their shaming targets what people do:** Barbara A. Babcock, "Pueblo Clowning and Pueblo Clay: From Icon to Caricature in Cochiti Figurative Ceramics, 1875–1900," in *Approaches to Iconology* (Leiden: E. J. Brill, 1988).

6 **shame is borne of the conflict:** Paul Gilbert, "Evolution, Social Roles, and the Differences in Shame and Guilt," *Social Research* 70, no. 4 (2003): 1205–30, http://www.jstor.org/stable/40971967.

7n *Understanding and Treating Chronic Shame:* P. A. DeYoung, *Understanding and Treating Chronic Shame: A Relational/Neurobiological Approach* (New York: Routledge, 2015).

11 **The movie struck a painful chord:** Frank Bruni, "Am I My Brother's Keeper?," *The New York Times*, May 12, 2002, https://www.nytimes.com/2002/05/12/magazine/am-i-my-brother-s-keeper.html.

12 **investigative series about abuse in the Catholic Church:** Thomas Farragher and Sacha Pfeiffer, "More Clergy Abuse, Secrecy Cases," *The Boston Globe*, May 1, 2012, https://www.bostonglobe.com/news/special-reports/2002/12/04/more-clergy-abuse-secrecy-cases/O5QkXOZG73XodDoX5hcPzJ/story.html.

Chapter 1: Tipping the Scales

26 **Florida State University study shows:** Angelina R. Sutin and Antonio Terracciano, "Perceived Weight Discrimination and Obesity,"

PLOS One 8, no. 7 (July 24, 2013), https://doi.org/10.1371/journal .pone.0070048.

26 **doctors "can't see past the fat":** Gina Kolata, "Why Do Obese Patients Get Worse Care? Many Doctors Don't See Past the Fat," *The New York Times,* September 25, 2016, https://www.nytimes.com/ 2016/09/26/health/obese-patients-health-care.html.

27 **UCLA researchers found:** Stuart Wolpert, "Dieting Does Not Work, UCLA Researchers Report," UCLA Newsroom, April 3, 2007, https://newsroom.ucla.edu/releases/Dieting-Does-Not-Work -UCLA-Researchers-7832.

27 **a monster $72 billion industry:** "The $72 Billion Weight Loss & Diet Control Market in the United States, 2019–2023," *Business Wire,* February 25, 2019, https://www.businesswire.com/news/home/ 20190225005455.

27 **adult obesity rate in the United States was 42.4 percent:** Matthew Rees, "'Hooked' Review, Lured into Gluttony," *The Wall Street Journal,* March 11, 2021, https://www.wsj.com/articles/hooked-review -lured-into-gluttony-11615505415.

27 **Even wild animals, by some accounts, are gaining weight:** Daniel Luzer, "It's Not Just All of the People around You That Are Getting Fatter," *Pacific Standard,* June 14, 2017, https://psmag.com/social -justice/just-people-getting-fatter-65342.

28 **"Genes load the gun, and environment pulls the trigger":** Joseph P. Williams, "Scientific, Societal Factors to Blame for Obesity Epidemic," *U.S. News & World Report,* May 16, 2019, https://www .usnews.com/news/healthiest-communities/articles/2019-05-16/ understanding-obesity-in-america.

28 **84 percent of the customers failed in their diets:** Jacques Peretti, "Fat Profits: How the Food Industry Cashed In on Obesity," *The Guardian,* August 7, 2013, https://www.theguardian.com/lifeandstyle/2013/ aug/07/fat-profits-food-industry-obesity.

28 **a prime example of such cherry-picking:** Susan A. Jebb et al., "Primary Care Referral to a Commercial Provider for Weight Loss Treatment versus Standard Care: A Randomised Controlled Trial," *The Lancet* 378, no. 9801 (October 22, 2011): 1485–92, https://doi.org/ 10.1016/S0140-6736(11)61344-5.

28 **earlier Weight Watchers research, published in 2008:** Michael R. Lowe, Tanja V. E. Kral, and Karen Miller-Kovach, "Weight-Loss

Maintenance 1, 2 and 5 Years after Successful Completion of a Weight-Loss Programme," *British Journal of Nutrition* 99, no. 4 (April 2008): 925–30, https://doi.org/10.1017/S0007114507862416.

29 **the company works this dreary fact into its pitch:** Kayla Reynolds, "Why Diets Don't Work," Noom, https://web.noom.com/blog/2016/12/diets-dont-work/.

30 **Noom cites its own study:** S. O. Chin et al., "Successful Weight Reduction and Maintenance by Using a Smartphone Application in Those with Overweight and Obesity," *Scientific Reports,* 6, no. 1 (2016), https://doi.org/10.1038/srep34563.

32 **she walked away with \$250,000 in prize money:** Alanna Nuñez, "Rachel Frederickson, The Biggest Loser, and Losing Weight Fast," *Shape,* April 3, 2014, https://www.shape.com/celebrities/rachel-frederickson-biggest-loser-and-losing-weight-fast.

32 **four of the fourteen studied were heavier six years later:** Gina Kolata, "After 'The Biggest Loser,' Their Bodies Fought to Regain Weight," *The New York Times,* May 2, 2016, https://www.nytimes.com/2016/05/02/health/biggest-loser-weight-loss.html.

32 **"Why are we celebrating her body?":** A. Chiu, "Jillian Michaels Asked Why People Are 'Celebrating' Lizzo's Body. Critics Slammed Her as 'Fatphobic,'" *The Washington Post,* January 9, 2020, https://www.washingtonpost.com/nation/2020/01/09/jillian-michaels-lizzo-fat-shaming/.

34 **more likely to struggle with their weight:** Jerica M. Berge et al., "Cumulative Encouragement to Diet from Adolescence to Adulthood: Longitudinal Associations with Health, Psychosocial Well-Being, and Romantic Relationships," *Journal of Adolescent Health* 65, no. 5 (November 2019): 690–97, https://doi.org/10.1016/j.jadohealth.2019.06.002.

Chapter 2: Shifting the Blame

37 **an endless cycle of jail and failed rehab:** Annie Broughton, "Blossom Rogers, Michelle Roberson, Sherry Anne, Part 1," *Florida Nite Line,* April 4, 2018, https://www.youtube.com/watch?v=WEiDg5187bc.

37 **teenage mother in New Smyrna Beach:** Cornelius Stafford, *Testify: Journey from Detour to Destiny; Five Stories of Transforming Life's Tragedies into Life's Triumphs* (CS Inspires Productions, 2017).

38 **more likely to engage in problem drinking:** Matt Treeby and Rai-
mondo Bruno, "Shame and Guilt-Proneness: Divergent Impli-
cations for Problematic Alcohol Use and Drinking to Cope with
Anxiety and Depression Symptomatology," *Personality and Individual Differences* 53, no. 5 (October 2012): 613–17, https://doi.org/10
.1016/j.paid.2012.05.011.

38 **a 2001 study of women in Alcoholics Anonymous:** Shelly A.
Wiechelt, "The Specter of Shame in Substance Misuse," *Substance
Use & Misuse* 42, no. 2–3 (2007): 399–409, https://doi.org/10.1080/
10826080601142196.

39 **deflecting their efforts to counteract the stereotypes:** Susan Kitch-
ens, "Shaming Smokers Can Backfire," *The Wall Street Journal,*
June 8, 2020, https://www.wsj.com/articles/shaming-smokers-can
-backfire-11591640792.

39 **"I liked everything about crack cocaine":** Blossom Rogers, interview
by the author, March 3, 2020.

40 **"Theirs will be a life of certain suffering":** Zoe Romanowsky, "What
Happened to the Crack Babies?," *Crisis Magazine,* April 20, 2010,
https://www.crisismagazine.com/2010/what-happened-to-the
-crack-babies.

40 **distributing drugs to an underage child:** Dorothy E. Roberts, "Punishing Drug Addicts Who Have Babies: Women of Color, Equality,
and the Right of Privacy," *Harvard Law Review* 104, no. 7 (May
1991): 1419–82.

41 **But crack, unlike alcohol, didn't alter their brains:** Michel Martin, "Crack Babies: Twenty Years Later," National Public Radio,
May 3, 2010, https://www.npr.org/templates/story/story.php?storyId
=126478643.

44 **"These women live in filth":** Craig S. Palosky, "Born to the Burden of
Crack," *The Boston Globe,* August 18, 1989.

44 **Prison, of course, cost even more:** "Annual Determination of Average Cost of Incarceration," *Federal Register,* April 30, 2018, https://
www.federalregister.gov/documents/2018/04/30/2018-09062/annual
-determination-of-average-cost-of-incarceration.

45 **more than $3 billion per year:** Kara Gotsch and Vinay Basti, "Capi-
talizing on Mass Incarceration: U.S. Growth in Private Prisons," The
Sentencing Project, August 2, 2018, https://www.sentencingproject

.org/publications/capitalizing-on-mass-incarceration-u-s-growth
-in-private-prisons/.

50 **"They are reckless criminals"**: Christopher Rowland, "Prescription Opioids Destroyed Families. Now, Victims Worry Addiction Stigma May Keep Them from Getting Justice," *The Washington Post*, December 2, 2019, https://www.washingtonpost.com/business/economy/prescription-opioids-destroyed-families-now-victims-worry-addiction-stigma-may-keep-them-from-getting-justice/2019/12/02/02f51c9e-0642-11ea-b17d-8b867891d39d_story.html.

51 **"significantly reduces illicit opioid use compared with non-drug approaches"**: "Medication-Assisted Treatment Improves Outcomes for Patients with Opioid Use Disorder," Pew Charitable Trusts, November 22, 2016, https://www.pewtrusts.org/en/research-and-analysis/fact-sheets/2016/11/medication-assisted-treatment-improves-outcomes-for-patients-with-opioid-use-disorder.

53 **they might hold up convenience stores or snatch purses**: "Security Officer Charged with Stealing Insulin from St. Louis Park Clinic," FOX 9 Minneapolis–St. Paul, July 25, 2019, https://www.fox9.com/news/security-officer-charged-with-stealing-insulin-from-st-louis-park-clinic.

53 **two-thirds of the jailed population is struggling with drug abuse or addiction**: Eric Westervelt, "County Jails Struggle with a New Role as America's Prime Centers for Opioid Detox," National Public Radio, April 24, 2019, https://www.npr.org/2019/04/24/716398909/county-jails-struggle-with-a-new-role-as-americas-prime-centers-for-opioid-detox.

55 **She got into trouble with the state licensing board**: The notice of hearing where Jennifer Warren's license was revoked mentions she "used and exploited her clients for her personal benefit"; see https://www.documentcloud.org/documents/4365410-Notice-of-Hearing-022212.html#document/p13/a404194.

55 **they would scream insults**: Amy Julia Harris and Shoshana Walter, "She Said She'd Free Them from Addiction. She Turned Them into Her Personal Servants," *Reveal*, May 21, 2018, https://revealnews.org/article/drug-users-got-exploited-disabled-patients-got-hurt-one-woman-benefited-from-it-all/.

Chapter 3: The Undeserving Poor

57 **"They want it to be difficult"**: Scott Hutchins, interview by the author, August 17, 2020.

61 **African Americans accounted for only 35 percent of welfare recipients**: Martin Gilens, *Why Americans Hate Welfare: Race, Media, and the Politics of Antipoverty Policy* (Chicago: University of Chicago Press, 1999).

61 **barely enough for rent in many American cities**: Shawn Fremstad, "The Official U.S. Poverty Rate Is Based on a Hopelessly Out-of-Date Metric," *The Washington Post*, September 16, 2019, https://www.washingtonpost.com/outlook/2019/09/16/official-us-poverty-rate-is-based-hopelessly-out-of-date-metric/.

61 **homelessness epidemic expanded during a period of economic boom**: Mihir Zaveri, "Number of Homeless Students Rises to New High, Report Says," *The New York Times*, February 2, 2020, https://www.nytimes.com/2020/02/03/us/Homeless-students-public-schools.html?smid=nytcore-ios-share.

63 **"made me feel as much shame as I did that day"**: Issac Bailey, "Stop Shaming Poor People for Being Poor," CNN Opinion, March 29, 2017, https://www.cnn.com/2017/03/29/opinions/stop-shaming-poor-for-being-poor-bailey/index.html.

63 **threw the food in the trash**: Bettina Elias Siegel, "Shaming Children so Parents Will Pay the School Lunch Bill," *The New York Times*, April 30, 2017, https://www.nytimes.com/2017/04/30/well/family/lunch-shaming-children-parents-school-bills.html.

63 **"I need lunch money"**: Ivana Hrynkiw, "'I Need Lunch Money,' Alabama School Stamps on Child's Arm," *Birmingham Real-Time News*, March 7, 2019, https://www.al.com/news/birmingham/2016/06/gardendale_elementary_student.html.

64 **poverty may be even more shameful than sexual impotence**: Neal Gabler, "The Secret Shame of Middle-Class Americans," *The Atlantic*, May 2016, https://www.theatlantic.com/magazine/archive/2016/05/my-secret-shame/476415/.

64 **Withdrawal deepens as it leads to more poverty and shame**: Arnoud Plantinga and Seger M. Breugelmans, "Shame in Poverty and Social Withdrawal," Open Science Framework, March 2017, https://

www.arnoudplantinga.nl/pdf/Shame%20in%20Poverty%20and%20 Social%20Withdrawal.pdf.

66 "a second chance, not a way of life": Jordan Weissmann, "The Failure of Welfare Reform," *Slate,* June 1, 2016, https://slate.com/news-and -politics/2016/06/how-welfare-reform-failed.html.

66 the so-called Earned Income Tax Credit: "Policy Basics: The Earned Income Tax Credit," Center on Budget and Policy Priorities, December 10, 2019, https://www.cbpp.org/research/federal-tax/policy -basics-the-earned-income-tax-credit.

67 When Clinton's reforms were introduced in 1996: Lloyd Doggett, "Rep. Doggett: It's Time to Fix the Broken Welfare System," TalkPoverty, April 22, 2016, https://talkpoverty.org/2016/08/22/rep -doggett-time-fix-broken-welfare-system/.

67 that the number of American households living in the deepest poverty: "What Is 'Deep Poverty'?," Center for Poverty & Inequality Research, University of California, Davis, January 16, 2018, https:// poverty.ucdavis.edu/faq/what-deep-poverty.

68 "reduce their employment by at least one hour per week": Angela Rachidi, "How Would a Child Allowance Affect Unemployment?," American Enterprise Institute, February 8, 2021, https:// www.aei.org/poverty-studies/how-would-a-child-allowance-affect -employment/.

68 "CEO's mission is grounded": GuideStar Profile, Center for Employment Opportunities, Inc., https://www.guidestar.org/profile/13 -3843322.

69 "They slotted me to a job": Duane Townes, interview by the author, April 11, 2020.

70 "You're not thinking about the money": David Robinson, interview by the author, April 9, 2020.

70 wrote a glowing report on CEO: Cindy Redcross et al., "More Than a Job: Final Results from the Evaluation of the Center for Employment Opportunities (CEO) Transitional Jobs Program," MDRC, OPRE Report 2011–18, January 2012, https://www.mdrc.org/sites/ default/files/full_451.pdf.

71 "it seems certain he would have been": Tamir Rosenblum, email to the author, April 3, 2020.

72 discrimination based on their record: Dallas Augustine, Noah

Zatz, and Naomi Sugie, "Why Do Employers Discriminate against People with Records?," UCLA Institute for Research on Labor and Employment, July 2020, https://irle.ucla.edu/wp-content/uploads/2020/07/Criminal-Records-Final-6.pdf.

72 **pressure to accept work based on the threat from their parole officers:** Erin Hatton, ed., *Labor and Punishment: Work in and out of Prison* (Oakland: University of California Press, 2021).

73 **That way, CEO keeps its pipeline full:** The company insists that it complies with all wage and hour laws and that "CEO has worked to develop and refine an evidence-based program model which has consistently demonstrated reductions in recidivism in high-quality studies."They encourage readers to visit their website (ceoworks.org) to read their reports.

74 **attempted to gauge young children's capacity to master self-control:** Y. Shoda, W. Mischel, and P. K. Peake, "Predicting Adolescent Cognitive and Self-Regulatory Competencies from Preschool Delay of Gratification: Identifying Diagnostic Conditions," *Developmental Psychology* 26, no. 6 (1990): 978–86, https://doi.org/10.1037/0012-1649 .26.6.978.

75 **"But fools gulp theirs down":** Proverbs 21:20 (New International Version).

75 **while controlling for the parents' income and education:** Tyler W. Watts, Greg J. Duncan, and Haonan Quan, "Revisiting the Marshmallow Test: A Conceptual Replication Investigating Links between Early Delay of Gratification and Later Outcomes," *Psychological Science* 29, no. 7 (2018): 1159–77, https://journals.sagepub.com/doi/10 .1177/0956797618761661.

Chapter 4: "Your Vagina Is Fine"

77 **"It wasn't that I didn't know about feminine hygiene":** Krista Torres, "It Used to Be Common for Women to Use Lysol to Clean Their Vagina and Here's Why," BuzzFeed, May 22, 2020, https://www .buzzfeed.com/kristatorres/women-used-to-wash-their-vaginas -with-lysol-so-heres-how-an.

78 **vain hope that the germ killer would work as a contraceptive:** Rose Eveleth, "Lysol's Vintage Ads Subtly Pushed Women to Use Its Disinfectant as Birth Control," *Smithsonian*, September 30, 2013,

https://www.smithsonianmag.com/smart-news/lysols-vintage-ads
-subtly-pushed-women-to-use-its-disinfectant-as-birth-control
-218734/.

78 **a tenfold increase over the past two decades:** Robert H. Shmerling, "FDA Curbs Unfounded Memory Supplement Claims," Harvard Health Blog, May 31, 2019, https://www.health.harvard.edu/blog/ fda-curbs-unfounded-memory-supplement-claims-2019053116772.

79 **"taps into a primal fear about reproductive tract cleanliness":** Jen Gunter, "Merchants of Shame," *The Vajenda*, February 24, 2021, https://vajenda.substack.com/p/merchants-of-shame.

80 **"Vaginal odor happens":** Vagisil, "In the Know: Vaginal Odor," https://www.vagisil.com/health-guide/vaginal-odor.

80 **they can even attack odor before it gets started:** https://www.vagisil .com/products.

80 **Gunter argues that women risk damaging themselves:** https:// drjengunter.com/.

80 **the safest approach is to stick with water:** Gunter, "Merchants of Shame."

81 **"Your vagina is fine":** Jocelyn J. Fitzgerald (@jfitzgeraldMD), Twitter, February 6, 2021, https://twitter.com/jfitzgeraldMD/status/ 1358083328864354310.

82 **Kardashian's fortune was creeping toward billionaire status:** Marissa DeSantis, "Kardashian Rich List: From Kim Kardashian Reaching Billionaire Status to Kylie's *Actual* Net Worth," *Evening Standard*, September 10, 2020, https://www.standard.co.uk/insider/celebrity/ kardashian-family-net-worth-a4484961.html.

83 **this number explodes to 78 percent by the time they reach seventeen:** Heather R. Gallivan, "Teens, Social Media and Body Image," Park Nicollet Melrose Center, Spring 2014, https://www.macmh .org/wp-content/uploads/2014/05/18_Gallivan_Teens-social-media -body-image-presentation-H-Gallivan-Spring-2014.pdf.

84 **estimated value of $250 million in 2019:** David Gelles, "Gwyneth Paltrow Is All Business," *The New York Times*, March 6, 2019, https:// www.nytimes.com/2019/03/06/business/gwyneth-paltrow-goop -corner-office.html.

85 **"engineers are getting Botox":** Ashton Applewhite, interview by the author, November 19, 2018.

86 **"make a totally obnoxious amount of money":** Chiara Eisner,

"Americans Took Prevagen for Years—as the FDA Questioned Its Safety," *Wired*, October 21, 2020, https://www.wired.com/story/prevagen-made-millions-fda-questioned-safety/.

86 **"will restore for you the lost protein"**: "FDA Warning Letter to Quincy Bioscience," Casewatch, Quackwatch, October 16, 2012, https://quackwatch.org/cases/fdawarning/prod/fda-warning-letters-about-products-2012/quincy/.

87 **"if apoaequorin is so great, why aren't jellyfish smarter?"**: Shmerling, "FDA Curbs Unfounded Memory Supplement Claims."

87 **"[a] large double blind, placebo-controlled trial"**: Federal Trade Commission and People of the State of New York v. Quincy Bioscience Holding Company, Inc., case 17-3745, March 5, 2018, https://www.ftc.gov/system/files/documents/cases/quincy_bioscience_ca2_ftc_brief_special_appendix_2018-0228.pdf.

87 **According to the FTC's complaint against Prevagen**: Megan L. Head et al., "The Extent and Consequences of P-Hacking in Science," *PLOS Biology* 13, no. 3 (2015), https://doi.org/10.1371/journal.pbio.1002106.

88 **They showed no statistically significant improvement**: Federal Trade Commission, case 17-3745.

89 **The psychologist Donna Hicks**: D. Hicks and D. Tutu, *Dignity: The Essential Role It Plays in Resolving Conflict* (New Haven, Conn.: Yale University Press, 2011).

Chapter 5: Click on Conflict

95 **"I thought nothing of it"**: Jennifer Knapp Wilkinson, "'My 15 Minutes of Fame': What Happened When a Cruel Photo of Me Went Viral," Today.com, January 30, 2017, https://www.today.com/health/my-15-minutes-fame-what-happened-when-cruel-photo-me-t107163.

96 **The reward circuits in the striatum**: Molly Crockett, interview by the author, October 16, 2020.

97n **For more examples of viral and international shaming**: Jon Ronson, *So You've Been Publicly Shamed* (New York: Picador, 2015).

98 **"Have you ever seen a more punchable face than this kid's?"**: Evan Gerstmann, "The Level of Violent Imagery Directed against Covington High Boys Is Dangerous and Wrong," *Forbes*, January 24,

2019, https://www.forbes.com/sites/evangerstmann/2019/01/24/the-level-of-violent-imagery-directed-against-covington-high-boys-is-dangerous-and-wrong/.

98 **Laura Ingraham urged Twitter:** "Multiple Investigations into Twitter Users Making Terroristic Threats against Covington Students," Fox News, January 23, 2019, https://www.foxnews.com/transcript/report-multiple-investigations-into-twitter-users-making-terroristic-threats-against-covington-students.

99 **a social and political Rorschach test:** Zack Beauchamp, "The Real Politics behind the Covington Catholic Controversy, Explained," *Vox,* January 23, 2019, https://www.vox.com/policy-and-politics/2019/1/23/18192831/covington-catholic-maga-hat-native-american-nathan-phillips.

100 **"they watch as if they're in a wrestling booth at a fair":** Julian Barnes, *The Man in the Red Coat* (New York: Knopf, 2020).

100 **"more and more divisive content":** Jeff Horwitz and Deepa Seetharaman, "Facebook Executives Shut Down Efforts to Make the Site Less Divisive," *The Wall Street Journal,* May 26, 2020, https://www.wsj.com/articles/facebook-knows-it-encourages-division-top-executives-nixed-solutions-11590507499.

101 **"dangerous (and life-threatening) real-world consequences":** Laura W. Murphy, "Facebook's Civil Rights Audit," July 8, 2020, https://about.fb.com/wp-content/uploads/2020/07/Civil-Rights-Audit-Final-Report.pdf.

103 **government-sanctioned social credit scores:** Nadra Nittle, "Spend 'Frivolously' and Be Penalized under China's New Social Credit System," *Vox,* November 2, 2018, https://www.vox.com/the-goods/2018/11/2/18057450/china-social-credit-score-spend-frivolously-video-games.

105 **struggled mightily to remove his (false) arrest record from the internet:** Sarah Esther Lageson, "There's No Such Thing as Expunging a Criminal Record Anymore," *Slate,* January 7, 2019, https://slate.com/technology/2019/01/criminal-record-expungement-internet-due-process.html.

107 **"This app really helps flaunt":** Body Tune, Slim & Skinny Photo Reviews 2021, https://justuseapp.com/en/app/1222515036/body-tune-slim-skinny-photo/reviews.

Chapter 6: Humiliation and Defiance

110n **she is suing her former employer:** Merrit Kennedy, "Fired after Calling 911 on a Black Bird-Watcher, Amy Cooper Sues for Discrimination," National Public Radio, May 27, 2021, https://www.npr.org/2021/05/27/1000831280/amy-cooper-911-call-black-bird-watcher-lawsuit.

111n **the 2014 app SketchFactor:** Andrew Marantz, "When an App Is Called Racist," *The New Yorker,* July 29, 2015, https://www.newyorker.com/business/currency/what-to-do-when-your-app-is-racist.

112 **a flood would drown humanity:** Leon Festinger, Henry W. Riecken, and Stanley Schachter, *When Prophecy Fails* (Minneapolis: University of Minnesota Press, 1956).

114 **"Stick a fork in her. She's done":** @MizFlagPin, Twitter, July 1, 2020, https://twitter.com/MizFlagPin/status/1278178042171572224.

115 **"bowing to cancel culture":** Ben Mathis-Lilley, "Andrew Cuomo Blames 'Cancel Culture' for Dozens of Accounts of Him Being a Lying, Obnoxious Creep," *Slate,* March 12, 2021, https://slate.com/news-and-politics/2021/03/andrew-cuomo-wont-resign-blames-cancel-culture-for-reports-hes-a-lying-obnoxious-creep.html.

116 **"lets white people off the hook":** Christian Cooper, "Opinion: Christian Cooper: Why I Have Chosen Not to Aid the Investigation of Amy Cooper," *The Washington Post,* July 14, 2020, https://www.washingtonpost.com/opinions/christian-cooper-why-I-am-declining-to-be-involved-in-amy-coopers-prosecution/2020/07/14/1ba3a920-c5d4-11ea-b037-f9711f89ee46_story.html.

117 **the mythology of the South's Lost Cause:** Bennett Minton, "The Lies Our Textbooks Told My Generation of Virginians about Slavery," *The Washington Post,* July 31, 2020, https://www.washingtonpost.com/outlook/slavery-history-virginia-textbook/2020/07/31/d8571eda-d1f0-11ea-8c55-61e7fa5e82ab_story.html.

119 **"might set them free from being white":** Eddie S. Glaude, Jr., "Blaming Trump Is Too Easy: This Is Us," Deadline White House, August 5, 2019, https://www.msnbc.com/deadline-white-house/watch/blaming-trump-is-too-easy-this-is-us-65354309615.

119 **the battle over a racial reckoning:** E. Pendharkar, "A $5 Million Fine for Classroom Discussions on Race? In Tennessee, This Is the New Reality," *Education Week,* August 4, 2021, https://www.edweek.org/

leadership/a-5-million-fine-for-classroom-discussions-on-race-in
-tennessee-this-is-the-new-reality/2021/08.

120 **"scapegoating must remain unconscious"**: Martin Berny, "The Hollywood Indian Stereotype: The Cinematic Othering and Assimilation of Native Americans at the Turn of the 20th Century," *Angles,* October 2020, https://doi.org/10.4000/angles/331.

122 **to move the homeless into her neighborhood**: Gwynne Hogan and Jake Offenhartz, "Angry Upper West Siders Wanted Homeless 'Scum' Out of Their Neighborhood. De Blasio Took Their Side," *Gothamist,* September 11, 2020, https://gothamist.com/news/angry-upper-west
-siders-wanted-homeless-scum-out-their-neighborhood-de-blasio
-took-their-side.

126 **"The bedbugs are Bret Stephens"**: Dave Karpf (@davekarpf), Twitter, August 26, 2019, https://twitter.com/davekarpf/status/11660949
50024515584.

126 **"dehumanizing and totally unacceptable"**: Hannah Knowles, "Bret Stephens Is Still Talking about Bedbugs—and Now, the Language of the Holocaust," *The Washington Post,* August 31, 2019, https://www
.washingtonpost.com/arts-entertainment/2019/08/31/bret-stephens
-is-still-talking-about-bedbugs-now-language-holocaust/.

127 **"rodents, insects and garbage"**: Bret Stephens, "World War II and the Ingredients of Slaughter," *The New York Times,* August 30, 2019, https://www.nytimes.com/2019/08/30/opinion/world-war-ii
-anniversary.html.

127 **"to threaten random Twitter users"**: David Karpf, "Op-Ed: I Made a Joke about Bret Stephens and Bedbugs. His Response Was Never about Civility," *Los Angeles Times,* August 28, 2019, https://www
.latimes.com/opinion/story/2019-08-28/bedbug-bret-stephens
-twitter-speech-civility-new-york-times.

128 **"the story went immediately viral"**: Karpf, "I Made a Joke about Bret Stephens."

128 **"The democratic inclusion we want"**: "A Letter on Justice and Open Debate," *Harper's Magazine,* August 21, 2020, https://harpers.org/a
-letter-on-justice-and-open-debate/.

128n **The singer Barbra Streisand gave birth to this effect**: Stacy Conradt, "How Barbra Streisand Inspired the 'Streisand Effect,'" *Mental Floss,* August 18, 2015, https://www.mentalfloss.com/article/67299/
how-barbra-streisand-inspired-streisand-effect.

130 **too many of the presumed powerless were speaking up:** Jennifer Schuessler and Elizabeth A. Harris, "Artists and Writers Warn of an 'Intolerant Climate.' Reaction Is Swift," *The New York Times,* July 7, 2020, https://www.nytimes.com/2020/07/07/arts/harpers-letter.html.

131 **"So who's trying to silence who?":** DMP from Pennsylvania. Comment on: Schuessler and Harris, "Artists and Writers Warn of an 'Intolerant Climate.' Reaction Is Swift." Comment posted July 8, 2020.

131 **"segregation now, segregation tomorrow and segregation forever":** "'Segregation Forever': A Fiery Pledge Forgiven, but Not Forgotten," *All Things Considered,* Radio Diaries, National Public Radio, January 10, 2013, https://www.npr.org/2013/01/14/169080969/segregation-forever-a-fiery-pledge-forgiven-but-not-forgotten.

132 **"something he had never done for anyone else":** Jonathan Capehart, "Opinion: How Segregationist George Wallace Became a Model for Racial Reconciliation," episode 6 of "Voices of the Movement," *The Washington Post,* May 16, 2019, https://www.washingtonpost.com/opinions/2019/05/16/changed-minds-reconciliation-voices-movement-episode/.

133 **"I can only ask for your forgiveness":** Capehart, "How Segregationist George Wallace Became a Model for Racial Reconciliation."

Chapter 7: Rejection and Denial

136 **"For the last eight years of my life":** "Retribution," YouTube, May 24, 2014, *The New York Times,* https://www.nytimes.com/video/us/100000002900707/youtube-video-retribution.html.

137 **police attributed at least forty-seven:** Dean C. Alexander and Dominic Lesniewski, "The Violent Fringe of the Incel Movement," Police1, Lexipol, September 19, 2019, https://www.police1.com/mass-casualty/articles/the-violent-fringe-of-the-incel-movement-M2E5r1B5BYTDesoL/.

138 **"It's like a game of one-upmanship":** Bradley Hinds, interviews by the author, August 7 and August 17, 2020.

140 **According to a 2018** *Washington Post* **survey:** "Demographics of Inceldom," Incels Wiki, June 7, 2021.

140 **linguistic analysis of forty-nine thousand postings:** Sylvia Jaki et

al., "Online Hatred of Women in the Incels.me Forum: Linguistic Analysis and Automatic Detection," *Journal of Language Aggression and Conflict* 7, no. 2 (2019): 240–68, https://doi.org/10.1075/jlac .00026.jak.

141 **"Mate choice is a difficult problem":** "Joe Rogan—Jordan Peterson Clarifies His Incels Comment," YouTube, July 2018, JRE Clips, https://www.youtube.com/watch?v=jsMqSBB3ZTY.

142 **Following his discussion of enforced monogamy:** Nellie Bowles, "Jordan Peterson, Custodian of the Patriarchy," *The New York Times,* May 18, 2018, https://www.nytimes.com/2018/05/18/style/jordan -peterson-12-rules-for-life.html.

142 **sex as a welfare benefit:** Robin Hanson, "Two Types of Envy," Overcoming Bias, April 26, 2018, https://www.overcomingbias.com/2018/ 04/two-types-of-envy.html.

145 **expanding available inventory to incels:** Nellie Bowles, "'Replacement Theory,' a Racist, Sexist Doctrine, Spreads in Far-Right Circles," *The New York Times,* March 18, 2019, https://www.nytimes .com/2019/03/18/technology/replacement-theory.html.

145 **historically, the majority of hikikomori have been men:** Cristian Martini Grimaldi, "The Social Suicide of Japan's 'Hikikomori,'" UCA News, December 28, 2020, https://www.ucanews.com/news/ the-social-suicide-of-japans-hikikomori/90827#.

146 **"having betrayed their parents' expectations":** Sekiguchi Hiroshi, "Islands of Solitude: A Psychiatrist's View of the Hikikomori," Nippon.com, December 13, 2017.

147 *hikidashiya,* **or "those who pull people out":** Gavin Blair, "In Japan, Extreme Bids to Help Hikikomori Are Causing Them Further Distress," *South China Morning Post,* June 27, 2020, https://www.scmp .com/week-asia/people/article/3090786/japan-extreme-bids-help -hikikomori-are-causing-them-further.

147 **A complaint to Tokyo police in 2020:** Blair, "In Japan, Extreme Bids to Help Hikikomori."

149 **the sociologist Michael Kimmel provides:** Michael S. Kimmel, "The Making—and Unmaking—of Violent Men," in *Healing from Hate: How Young Men Get into—and out of—Violent Extremism* (Oakland: University of California Press, 2018), 1–27.

Chapter 8: The Common Good

153 **"There is some degree of opprobrium if one does not wear it in certain settings"**: Robert Barnes et al., "Supreme Court Appears Ready to Uphold Affordable Care Act over Latest Challenge from Trump, GOP," *The Washington Post,* November 10, 2020, https:// www.washingtonpost.com/politics/2020/11/10/scotus-hearing-aca -live-updates/.

155 **"We are desperate for an outlet"**: Amanda Hess, "The Social-Distancing Shamers Are Watching," *The New York Times,* May 11, 2020, https://www.nytimes.com/2020/05/11/arts/social-distance -shaming.html.

155 **"Stay home and stay muzzled"**: sonia (@soniapatriot), Twitter, June 26, 2020.

155 **the only person at a party to wear a mask**: Robert L. Klitzman, "If You See Someone Not Wearing a Mask, Do You Say Something?," *The New York Times,* September 10, 2020, https://www.nytimes.com/ 2020/09/10/well/live/mask-shaming.html.

156 **At a contentious meeting**: Annie Gowen, "'God Be with Us,'" *The Washington Post,* December 9, 2020, https://www.washingtonpost .com/nation/2020/12/09/south-dakota-mitchell-covid-masks/.

156 **Crews lambasted the people mandating masks**: J. Clara Chan, "NIH Official to Retire after He's Exposed as RedState Editor Who Called Fauci a 'Mask Nazi,'" TheWrap, September 21, 2020, https://www.thewrap.com/nih-official-to-retire-after-hes-exposed -as-redstate-editor-who-called-fauci-a-mask-nazi/.

158 **"people who get COVID-19 have behaved irresponsibly"**: Alain Labrique et al., "Webinar: National Pandemic Pulse Round 1," covidinequities.org, November 12, 2020, https://www.covidinequities .org/post/webinar-national-pandemic-pulse-round-1.

159 **smallpox was much more deadly**: Stefan Riedel, "Edward Jenner and the History of Smallpox Vaccination," *Baylor University Medical Center Proceedings* 18, no. 1 (2005), https://www.tandfonline.com/ doi/abs/10.1080/08998280.2005.11928028.

161 **a debunked and retracted 1998 paper**: A. Sabra, J. A. Bellanti, and A. R. Colón, "Ileal-Lymphoid-Nodular Hyperplasia, Non-Specific Colitis, and Pervasive Developmental Disorder in Children," *The*

Lancet, 352, no. 9123 (1998): 234–35, https://doi.org/10.1016/s0140 -6736(05)77837-5.

162 **many African Americans, for example, are skeptical of vaccines:** Saundra Young, "Black Vaccine Hesitancy Rooted in Mistrust, Doubts, WebMD, February 2, 2021, https://www.webmd.com/ vaccines/covid-19-vaccine/news/20210202/black-vaccine-hesitancy -rooted-in-mistrust-doubts.

162 **leaving hundreds untreated for syphilis:** "The Tuskegee Timeline," Centers for Disease Control and Prevention, April 22, 2021, https:// www.cdc.gov/tuskegee/timeline.htm.

162 **a standard line for oncology research:** "Henrietta Lacks: Science Must Right a Historical Wrong," editorial, *Nature* 585, no. 7 (September 2020), https://www.nature.com/articles/d41586-020-02494-z.

162 **Hasidic Jews in New York:** H. Dreyfus, "Why Some Orthodox Jewish Women Won't Get Vaccinated," *The New York Times*, June 11, 2021, https://www.nytimes.com/2021/06/11/nyregion/orthodox-jewish -vaccinations.html.

163 **angry Hasidic men burned their masks:** T. Armus, "Brooklyn's Orthodox Jews Burn Masks in Violent Protests as New York Cracks Down on Rising Coronavirus Cases," *The Washington Post*, October 8, 2020, https://www.washingtonpost.com/nation/2020/10/08/ orthodox-jews-protest-covid-brooklyn/.

163 **"There's an anti-authority feeling in the world":** I. Derysh, "Fauci 'Absolutely Not' Surprised Trump Got COVID: He 'Equates Wearing a Mask with Weakness,'" *Salon*, October 19, 2020, https://www .salon.com/2020/10/19/fauci-absolutely-not-surprised-trump-got -covid-he-equates-wearing-a-mask-with-weakness/.

163 **The plaintiffs argued that the vaccines were an experimental therapy:** Derek Hawkins, "117 Staffers Sue over Houston Hospital's Vaccine Mandate, Saying They Don't Want to Be 'Guinea Pigs,'" *The Washington Post*, May 30, 2021, https://www.washingtonpost.com/ nation/2021/05/29/texas-hospital-vaccine-lawsuit/.

164 **some of her colleagues objected to the frantic pace of the vaccine development:** Kristen Choi (@kristenrchoi), "I'm often asked 'Why are so many nurses declining the COVID vaccine?'— & I'm usually unsure how to respond. I'm torn between being embarrassed/upset by low vaccine uptake among nurses or sympathetic to the reasons

why nurses don't automatically trust hospitals & biomedicine. 🗿⬇️," Twitter, April 9, 2021, https://twitter.com/kristenrchoi/status/1380705692684754945.

164 **pandemic deniers at a California hot yoga studio:** Stephanie Sierra, "Pacifica Yoga Studio Continues to Hold 'Mask Free, Virus Free' Classes, Prompts New Investigation," ABC7 San Francisco, KGO-TV, December 20, 2020, https://abc7news.com./pacifica-beach-yoga -bay-area-indoor-classes-studio-defies-covid-19-order-san-mateo -health-noncompliance/8910067/.

164 **"So think of vaccines as part of God's plan":** Jan Hoffman, "Clergy Preach Faith in the Covid Vaccine to Doubters," *The New York Times,* March 14, 2021, https://www.nytimes.com/2021/03/14/health/clergy -covid-vaccine.html.

164 **"not only because of our best interest":** Katie Jackson, "For Gathering Safely with Her Congregation and Traveling: Pastor Gets COVID-19 Vaccine," WellSpan Health, May 21, 2021, https://www.wellspan .org/news/story/for-gathering-safely-with-her-congregation-and -traveling-pastor-gets-covid-19-vaccine/N6392.

Chapter 9: Punching Up

169 **"to shame [America]":** Frederick Douglass, letter, Glasgow (Scotland), April 15, 1846. To Horace Greeley. Philip Foner, ed., *Life and Writings of Frederick Douglass,* vol. 1 (New York: International Publishers, 1950), 144.

169n **more positive use of shame:** Jennifer Jacquet, *Is Shame Necessary? New Uses for an Old Tool* (New York: Vintage, 2016).

171 **The doctors used cellphone lights:** Chukwuemeka Anyikwa, "End Sars Protests: Why Anthony Unuode Gave His Life for a Better Nigeria," BBC News, November 3, 2020, https://www.bbc.com/news/world-africa-54747916.

171 **"We have no other motive":** M. Buhari, "The hard work to deliver a better Nigeria continues, building on the foundations of peace, rule of law and opportunities for all. We have no other motive than to serve Nigeria with our hearts and might, and build a nation which we and generations to come can be proud of," pic.twitter.com/EoO5To78mL, Twitter, https://mobile.twitter.com/mbuhari/status/1100797066391867392?lang=bg.

174 **"shake the British Empire"**: "Gandhi's Salt March, the Tax Protest That Changed Indian History," https://www.history.co.uk/article/gandhis-salt-march-the-tax-protest-that-changed-indian-history.

175 **"They went down like ten-pins"**: Whitney Sanford, "What Gandhi Can Teach Today's Protesters," ed. Beth Daley, The Conversation, October 1, 2017, https://theconversation.com/what-gandhi-can-teach-todays-protesters-83404.

175 **"inflicted such humiliation and defiance"**: E. Andrews, "When Gandhi's Salt March Rattled British Colonial Rule," *The Daily Star*, March 14, 2021, https://www.thedailystar.net/in-focus/news/when-gandhis-salt-march-rattled-british-colonial-rule-2060665.

176 **he in turn called them "sissies"**: Daniel Lewis, "Larry Kramer, Playwright and Outspoken AIDS Activist, Dies at 84," *The New York Times*, May 27, 2020, https://www.nytimes.com/2020/05/27/us/larry-kramer-dead.html.

177 *"you make decisions that cost the lives of others"*: Larry Kramer, "An Open Letter to Dr. Anthony Fauci," *The Village Voice*, May 31, 1988, https://www.villagevoice.com/2020/05/28/an-open-letter-to-dr-anthony-fauci/.

177 **"If you write a calm letter"**: Alex Witchel, "At Home With: Larry Kramer; When a Roaring Lion Learns to Purr," *The New York Times*, January 12, 1995, https://www.nytimes.com/1995/01/12/garden/at-home-with-larry-kramer-when-a-roaring-lion-learns-to-purr.html.

179 **"amazed and appalled" by the lack of civility**: Zack Beauchamp, "Sarah Sanders and the Failure of 'Civility,'" *Vox*, June 25, 2018, https://www.vox.com/policy-and-politics/2018/6/25/17499036/sarah-sanders-red-hen-restaurant-civility.

179 **"should be allowed to eat dinner in peace"**: E. Board, "Let the Trump Team Eat in Peace," *The Washington Post*, June 25, 2018, https://www.washingtonpost.com/opinions/let-the-trump-team-eat-in-peace/2018/06/24/46882e16-779a-11e8-80be-6d32e182a3bc_story.html.

180 **Never Again MSD**: @NeverAgainMSD, Facebook, February 15, 2018.

180 **being rejected by four universities**: Laura Ingraham (@Ingraham Angle), "David Hogg Rejected By Four Colleges To Which He Applied and whines about it. (Dinged by UCLA with a 4.1 GPA . . . totally predictable given acceptance rates.), https://t.co/

wflA4hWHXY," Twitter, March 28, 2018, https://twitter.com/ingrahamangle/status/979021639458459648?lang=en.

180 **urging his followers to shame them:** David Hogg (@davidhoggiii), "Pick a number 1-12 contact the company next to that # Top Laura Ingraham Advertisers: 1. @sleepnumber 2. @ATT 3. Nutrish 4. @Allstate & @esurance 5. @Bayer 6. @RocketMortgage Mortgage 7. @LibertyMutual 8. @Arbys 9. @TripAdvisor 10. @Nestle 11. @hulu 12. @Wayfair," Twitter, March 28, 2018, https://twitter.com/davidhoggiii/status/979168957180579840?lang=en.

180 **"On reflection, in the spirit of Holy Week":** E. Edwards, "3 Boston-Area Businesses Pull Ads from Fox News Show after David Hogg Comment," *The Daily Free Press*, April 4, 2018, https://dailyfreepress.com/2018/04/04/3-boston-area-businesses-pull-ads-from-fox-news-show-after-david-hogg-comment/.

180 **"@davidhoggiii is the real bully here! Shame!!":** @ChunkFlexi58, Twitter, n.d., accessed June 7, 2021. The original tweet and associated account no longer exist.

180 **the students organized a "die-in":** Nadeem Muaddi and Jamiel Lynch, "Publix Suspends Political Contributions following Criticism for Supporting Pro-NRA Candidate," CNN Politics, May 26, 2018, https://www.cnn.com/2018/05/25/politics/publix-putnam-hogg-protest/index.html.

181 **"In Parkland we will have a die in":** David Hogg (@davidhoggiii), ".@Publix is a #NRASellOut In Parkland we will have a die in the Friday (the 25th) before memorial day weekend. Starting at 4pm for 12 min inside our 2 Publix stores. Just go an lie down starting at 4. Feel free to die in with us at as many other @Publix as possible," Twitter, May 23, 2018, https://twitter.com/davidhoggiii/status/999288175511113729?lang=en.

181 **journalistic exposés of Harvey Weinstein:** R. Farrow, "From Aggressive Overtures to Sexual Assault: Harvey Weinstein's Accusers Tell Their Stories," *The New Yorker*, October 10, 2017, https://www.newyorker.com/news/news-desk/from-aggressive-overtures-to-sexual-assault-harvey-weinsteins-accusers-tell-their-stories.

183 **circulating among female colleagues stark naked:** Irin Carmon and Amy Brittain, "Eight Women Say Charlie Rose Sexually Harassed Them—with Nudity, Groping and Lewd Calls," *The Washington Post*, November 20, 2017, https://www.washingtonpost.com/

investigations/eight-women-say-charlie-rose-sexually-harassed
-them--with-nudity-groping-and-lewd-calls/2017/11/20/9b168de8
-caec-11e7-8321-481fd63f174d_story.html.

183 **there was a vast culling of men behaving badly:** Audrey Carlsen
et al., "#MeToo Brought Down 201 Powerful Men. Nearly Half of
Their Replacements Are Women," *The New York Times*, October 23,
2018, https://www.nytimes.com/interactive/2018/10/23/us/metoo
-replacements.html.

184 **46 percent felt angry, guilty, or persecuted:** Blair Rotstein, "How Do
Men Feel about #MeToo? Some Are Sad & Angry, Others Feel
'Nothing,'" *Flare*, February 28, 2018, https://www.flare.com/news/
how-do-men-feel-about-metoo/.

184 **"Rednecks made you a Millionaire!":** Carrie C (@brutalcountry),
"Hey, @adultswim and @cartoonnetwork, how do you feel about
this racist post from Squidbillies voice actor, #stuartbaker? Pic.twitter
.com/wWKIXAS9Uf," Twitter, August 13, 2020, https://twitter.com/
brutalcountry/status/1294098886617858049.

184 **"just tell me what else you want":** Tim Clodfelter, "'Squidbillies'
Drops Lead Actor after Controversial Posts," *Winston-Salem Journal*,
August 16, 2020, https://journalnow.com/entertainment/squidbillies
-drops-lead-actor-after-controversial-posts/article_7b41f368-e015
-11ea-980d-4f5a32112ada.html.

185 **"I'm remember[ing] you bastards!":** Andy Swift, "Fired Squidbillies
Star Sounds Off: 'I Hope You A—holes Are Happy,'" TVLine, August 18, 2020, https://tvline.com/2020/08/18/squidbillies-star-fired
-stuart-baker-response-controversy/.

186 **she had published a groundbreaking 2017 study:** Joy Buolamwini and
Timnit Gebru, "Gender Shades: Intersectional Accuracy Disparities
in Commercial Gender Classification," ed. Sorelle A. Friedler and
Christo Wilson, *Proceedings of Machine Learning Research* 81 (2018):
1–15, https://proceedings.mlr.press/v81/buolamwini18a/buolamwini18a
.pdf.

186 **led Amazon and Microsoft to stop selling the software to law enforcement:** Nitasha Tiku, "Google Hired Timnit Gebru to Be an
Outspoken Critic of Unethical AI. Then She Was Fired for It," *The
Washington Post*, December 23, 2020, https://www.washingtonpost
.com/technology/2020/12/23/google-timnit-gebru-ai-ethics/.

186 **"On the Dangers of Stochastic Parrots":** Karen Hao, "We Read

the Paper That Forced Timnit Gebru out of Google. Here's What It Says," *MIT Technology Review*, December 4, 2020, https://www.technologyreview.com/2020/12/04/1013294/google-ai-ethics-research-paper-forced-out-timnit-gebru/.

187 **she denounced the company for censoring her:** Casey Newton, "The Withering Email That Got an Ethical AI Researcher Fired at Google," Platformer, December 3, 2020, https://www.platformer.news/p/the-withering-email-that-got-an-ethical.

187 **"Don't be evil":** Larry W. Sonsini, David J. Segre, and William H. Hinman, Amendment No. 4 to Form S-1 Registration Statement, Google, July 26, 2004, https://www.sec.gov/Archives/edgar/data/1288776/000119312504124025/ds1a.htm.

188 **"research integrity and academic freedom":** "Standing with Dr. Timnit Gebru—#ISupportTimnit #BelieveBlackWomen," Google Walkout for Real Change, Medium, December 3, 2020, https://googlewalkout.medium.com/standing-with-dr-timnit-gebru-isupporttimnit-believeblackwomen-6dadc300d382.

188 **"I accept the responsibility of working to restore your trust":** Ina Fried, "Scoop: Google CEO Pledges to Investigate Exit of Top AI Ethicist," Axios, December 9, 2020, https://www.axios.com/sundar-pichai-memo-timnit-gebru-exit-18b0efb0-5bc3-41e6-ac28-2956732ed78b.html.

188 **one of her top collaborators, Margaret Mitchell, was let go:** Tom Simonite, "A Second AI Researcher Says She Was Fired by Google," *Wired*, February 19, 2021, https://www.wired.com/story/second-ai-researcher-says-fired-google/.

188 **The issues ranged from fairness to freedom and equality:** "On the Firing of Dr. Timnit Gebru," Google Docs, accessed June 7, 2021, https://docs.google.com/document/d/1ERi2crDToYhYjEjxRoOzO-uOUeLgdoLPfnxIJOErg2w/view.

188 **"I'm fired":** MMitchell (@mmitchell_ai), Twitter, February 19, 2021, https://twitter.com/mmitchell_ai/status/1362885356127801345?lang=en.

Chapter 10: Under the Knife

198 **a new diet he was on:** Mark Hyman, *The Eat Fat, Get Thin Cookbook: More Than 175 Delicious Recipes for Sustained Weight Loss and Vibrant Health* (New York: Little, Brown, 2016).

Conclusion

207 **save more lives than traditional methods:** Abby Goodnough, "This Addiction Treatment Works. Why Is It So Underused?," *The New York Times,* October 27, 2020, https://www.nytimes.com/2020/10/27/health/meth-addiction-treatment.html.

209 **"They probably were glad to make themselves useful":** "Milano-Tokyo Dialogue over Hikikomori," *Hikikomori News,* August 7, 2017, http://www.hikikomori-news.com/?p=2380.

212 **"to join an ongoing pile-on against a normal person":** Ezra Klein, "A Different Way of Thinking about Cancel Culture," *The New York Times,* April 18, 2021, https://www.nytimes.com/2021/04/18/opinion/cancel-culture-social-media.html.

213 **white cops defend a marauding colleague:** Jamil Zaki, *The War for Kindness: Building Empathy in a Fractured World* (New York: Crown, 2019), 134.

214 **"Forgiveness":** K. Thelwell, "9 inspiring Nelson Mandela quotes on forgiveness," The Borgen Project, November 5, 2019, https://borgenproject.org/nelson-mandela-quotes-on-forgiveness/.

215 **missteps shouldn't plunge us into everlasting shame:** In *Hiding from Humanity,* Martha C. Nussbaum masterfully argues against the explicit use of shame and disgust in our penal code on legal, moral, and ethical grounds. Martha C. Nussbaum, *Hiding from Humanity: Disgust, Shame, and the Law* (Princeton, N.J.: Princeton University Press, 2009).

INDEX

ABOUT THE AUTHOR

CATHY O'NEIL is the author of the bestselling *Weapons of Math Destruction*, which won the Euler Book Prize and was longlisted for the National Book Award. She received her PhD in mathematics from Harvard and has worked in finance, tech, and academia. She launched the Lede Program in Data Journalism at Columbia University and recently founded ORCAA, an algorithmic auditing company. O'Neil is a regular contributor to *Bloomberg View*.

Twitter: @mathbabedotorg

ABOUT THE TYPE

THIS BOOK WAS set in Caslon, a typeface first designed in 1722 by William Caslon (1692–1766). Its widespread use by most English printers in the early eighteenth century soon supplanted the Dutch typefaces that had formerly prevailed. The roman is considered a "work-horse" typeface due to its pleasant, open appearance, while the italic is exceedingly decorative.